ID0976820

Baking
Is
Fun

Volume 8

Recipes No. 594 - 678

Cover Recipe Pages 24 and 61

ISBN 0-9691357-8-5

Printed and Bound in Canada

Introduction

Dear Reader:

Congratulations on acquiring the 8th volume in our series, "Baking is Fun".

This book is specifically dedicated to cookies, because cookies are an honoured tradition in the Austrian kitchen. Most Austrian housewives have at least a few cookie recipes in their possession that have been lovingly passed from previous generations.

Cookies are not just favourites at Christmas time, but at any time. There is always an occasion to bring out these delightful delicacies. Baked ahead, cookies make an ideal coffee break sweet or tea time treat. Boxed or wrapped, they are also a thoughtful and much appreciated hostess gift.

We have carefully selected the recipes in this baking book for you. They have been divided into five chapters: delicious classic cookies, tea time pastries, festive treats, savoury biscuits and family favourites. There is something for every taste and temptation.

We wish you joyful baking and much success!

Additional copies of this book may be obtained by writing to:

oetker Recipe Service
2229 Drew Road
Mississauga, Ontario
L5S 1E5

Contents

Classic Cookies .... 6 - 33

Tea Time Pastries .... 34 - 55

Festive Treats .... 56 - 87

Savoury Biscuits .... 88 - 101

Family Favourites .... 102 - 123

Recipe Index .... 124 - 125

Personal Notes .... 126 - 127

The **oetker** Library of Baking 128

Classic Cookies

Choco-Walnut Macaroons

Recipe No. 594

Ingredients:

4	egg whites	4	
.5 mL	cream of tartar	$^1/_8$	tsp
50 g	sugar	$^1/_4$	cup
90 g	icing sugar, sifted	$^3/_4$	cup
1 mL	salt	$^1/_4$	tsp
4 drops	**oetker** vanilla flavouring concentrate	4	drops
60 g	walnuts, ground	$^2/_3$	cup

Cream Filling:

150 g	milk chocolate, chopped	6	squares
125 mL	whipping cream	$^1/_2$	cup

Decoration:

some	chocolate, melted	some	
some	pistachio nuts	some	

PREHEAT oven to 120°C (250°F). Line a baking sheet with parchment paper.
BEAT egg whites until frothy. Sift cream of tartar over surface, continue beating. Gradually beat in sugar and icing sugar.
CONTINUE beating until mass is stiff. Beat in salt and flavouring.
FOLD in walnuts.
DROP onto prepared baking sheet.
BAKE for 40-60 minutes.

Cream Filling:

PLACE chocolate in a saucepan. Add whipping cream.
STIRRING constantly, heat mixture over medium heat until chocolate has melted.
POUR mixture into mixing bowl. Chill.

Decoration:

USING an electric mixer, beat chilled mixture for 2-3 minutes.
SPREAD filling on the underside of half of the biscuits.
COVER with remaining biscuits.
DECORATE with melted chocolate and pistachio nuts.

Marzipan-Chocolate Slices

Recipe No. 595

Ingredients:

125	g	semi-sweet chocolate	4½ squares
90	g	icing sugar, sifted	¾ cup
255	g	marzipan	9 oz
2		egg whites	2
1	mL	cinnamon	¼ tsp

Brushing:

30	mL	honey	2 tbsp
15	mL	water	1 tbsp

PREHEAT oven to 150°C (300°F). Set aside two baking sheets. Line one with parchment paper.

SOFTEN chocolate in a double boiler. Pour into a mixing bowl.

ADD icing sugar, marzipan, egg whites and cinnamon.

BEAT approximately 5 minutes.

CHILL for one-half hour.

TURN mixture onto well-floured working surface.

ROLL out mixture. Place on unlined baking sheet.

PLACE in freezer for approximately 10 minutes.

USING a round cookie cutter, cut out slices 5 cm (2") in diameter.

PLACE slices on lined baking sheet. (Remove excess flour on the surface of the cookies with a small brush.)

BAKE for 20 minutes.

REMOVE from baking sheet.

COOL completely.

Brushing:

IN a small saucepan, combine honey and water. Bring to a boil. Brush warm honey mixture on the cookies.

*B*utter Cookies

Recipe No. 596

Dough:

375 g	all-purpose flour	2¾	cups
1 mL	**oetker** baking powder	¼	tsp
45 mL	**oetker** Gustin corn starch	3	tbsp
	pinch salt		pinch
230 g	icing sugar, sifted	2	cups
1 pkg	**oetker** vanilla sugar	1	pkg
5 drops	**oetker** lemon flavouring concentrate	5	drops
1	egg	1	
225 g	butter, cold	1	cup

Sprinkling:

some	icing sugar, sifted	some
some	cinnamon	some

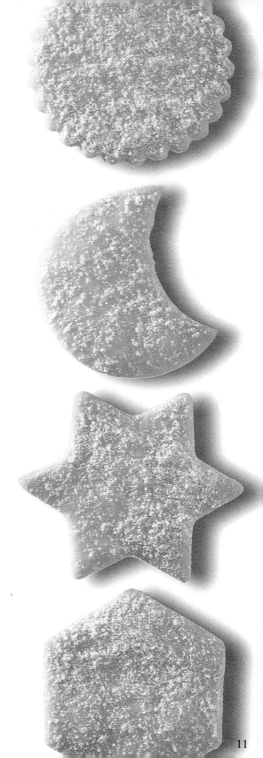

MIX together flour, baking powder and corn starch.
SIFT flour mixture onto a working surface.
MAKE a well in the centre. Put salt, icing sugar, vanilla sugar, flavouring and egg in the well.
CUT cold butter in small pieces over the ingredients in the well.
COVER with flour.
STARTING from the centre, work ingredients into a smooth dough.
CHILL for one hour.
PREHEAT oven to 190°C (375°F).
ROLL out dough thinly.
USING a variety of cutters, cut out shapes.
PLACE shapes on baking sheet.
BAKE for 10 minutes.

Sprinkling:
MIX together icing sugar and cinnamon.
SPRINKLE over hot cookies.

11

Lemony Butter Cookies

Recipe No. 597

Dough:

350 g	all-purpose flour	2¹/₂	cups
1 mL	**oetker** baking powder	¹/₄	tsp
	pinch salt		pinch
120 g	icing sugar, sifted	1	cup
1 pkg	**oetker** vanilla sugar	1	pkg
¹/₂ btl	**oetker** lemon flavouring concentrate	¹/₂	btl
15 mL	grated lemon peel, chopped	1	tbsp
275 g	butter or margarine, cold	1¹/₄	cups

Brushing:

1	egg	1	
45 mL	milk	3	tbsp

MIX together flour and baking powder.
SIFT onto a working surface.
MAKE a well in the centre. Put salt, icing sugar, vanilla sugar, flavouring and lemon peel in the well.
CUT cold butter or margarine in small pieces over the ingredients in the well.
COVER with flour.
STARTING from the centre, work ingredients into a smooth dough.
CHILL for one hour.
PREHEAT oven to 190°C (375°F).
ROLL out dough thinly.

Brushing:

WHISK together egg and milk.
BRUSH dough with egg mixture.
USING a fork, etch a pattern on the dough.
WITH a knife or cutters, cut out various shapes. Place shapes on baking sheet.
BAKE for 10 minutes.

Craquelins

Recipe No. 598

Dough:

250 g	all-purpose flour	1³/₄	cups
	pinch salt		pinch
50 g	icing sugar, sifted	¹/₂	cup
1 pkg	**oetker** vanilla sugar	1	pkg
1	egg	1	
30 mL	milk	2	tbsp
150 g	butter or margarine, cold	²/₃	cup

Brushing:

1	egg, whisked	1	

SIFT flour onto a working surface.
MAKE a well in the centre. Put salt, icing sugar, vanilla sugar, egg and milk in the well.
WORK into a thick paste.
CUT cold butter or margarine in small pieces over the flour mixture.
STARTING from the centre, work all ingredients into a smooth dough.
CHILL for one hour.
PREHEAT oven to 200°C (400°F).
ROLL out dough thinly.
USING a knife cut out squares in various sizes.
BRUSH with egg.
PLACE squares on baking sheet.
BAKE for 10-12 minutes.

Filled Lady Fingers

Recipe No. 599

Batter:

3	egg whites	3
50 g	sugar (first amount)	1/4 cup
1 pkg	**oetker** vanilla sugar	1 pkg
2 drops	**oetker** lemon flavouring concentrate	2 drops
125 mL	whipping cream	1/2 cup
50 g	sugar (second amount)	1/4 cup
100 g	all-purpose flour	3/4 cup

Cream Filling:

125 mL	whipping cream	1/2 cup
120 g	semi-sweet chocolate, chopped	4 1/2 squares
1 shot	Grand Marnier	1 shot

Glaze:

1 pkg	**oetker** Chocofix	1 pkg

PREHEAT oven to 200°C (400°F).
IN a mixing bowl, combine egg whites, sugar (first amount), vanilla sugar and flavouring.
BEAT to stiff peaks.
IN another bowl, combine whipping cream and sugar (second amount).
BEAT until mixture is of a thick consistency.
SPOON egg white mixture over cream mixture.
SIFT flour over entire mixture.
FOLD in gently but thoroughly.
PUT mixture into a pastry bag fitted with a small tube.
PIPE mixture in the shape of lady fingers, well apart, onto baking sheet.
BAKE for 8-10 minutes.
REMOVE lady fingers from baking sheet immediately.
COOL completely.

Cream Filling:

IN a saucepan, combine whipping cream, chocolate and Grand Marnier.
STIRRING constantly, heat mixture over medium heat until chocolate has melted.
POUR mixture into mixing bowl. Chill.
USING an electric mixer, beat chilled chocolate mixture for 2-3 minutes.
SPREAD filling on the underside of half of the lady fingers. Cover with remaining lady fingers.

Glaze:

SOFTEN Chocofix according to package directions.
HOLD each lady finger on an angle and dip into glaze.

Almond Boleros

Recipe No. 600

Dough:

250 g	all-purpose flour	1³/₄	cups
50 g	almonds, ground	¹/₂	cup
100 g	icing sugar, sifted	³/₄	cup
1 pkg	**oetker** vanilla sugar	1	pkg
1	egg	1	
5 drops	**oetker** almond flavouring concentrate	5	drops
150 g	butter or margarine, cold	²/₃	cup

Brushing:

1	egg, whisked	1	

Topping:

50 g	almonds, slivered	¹/₃	cup

SIFT flour onto a working surface.
ADD almonds and mix well.
MAKE a well in the centre. Put icing sugar,
vanilla sugar, egg and flavouring in the well.
CUT cold butter or margarine in small pieces
over the ingredients in the well.
STARTING from the centre, work all
ingredients into a smooth dough.
CHILL for one hour.
PREHEAT oven to 190°C (375°F).
ROLL out dough 3 mm (¹/₈") thick.
USING a scalloped cookie cutter, cut out
shapes 5 cm (2") in diameter.
PLACE shapes on baking sheet.
BRUSH with egg. Top with slivered almonds.
LIGHTLY press almonds into dough.
BAKE for 8-10 minutes.

Nougat Delights

Recipe No. 601

Dough:

400	g	all-purpose flour	3 cups
20	g	cocoa	¼ cup
1	mL	salt	¼ tsp
200	g	icing sugar, sifted	1¾ cups
1	pkg	**oetker** vanilla sugar	1 pkg
1		egg	1
300	g	butter or margarine, cold	1⅓ cups

Filling:

125	mL	vegetable oil	½ cup
90	g	icing sugar, sifted	¾ cup
1	pkg	**oetker** vanilla sugar	1 pkg
150	g	nougat	5 oz

MIX together flour and cocoa.
SIFT onto a working surface.
MAKE a well in the centre. Put salt, icing sugar, vanilla sugar and egg in the well.
CUT the cold butter or margarine into small pieces over the ingredients in the well.
STARTING from the centre, work all ingredients into a smooth dough.
SHAPE dough into rolls 5 cm (2") in diameter.
WRAP rolls in aluminum foil.
CHILL for two hours.
PREHEAT oven to 190°C (375°F).
REMOVE dough from foil.
CUT into slices 3 mm (⅛") thick.
PLACE slices on baking sheet.
BAKE for 12 minutes.

Filling:

IN a mixing bowl, combine oil, icing sugar and vanilla sugar.
BEAT until fluffy.
ADD nougat. Mix well.
SPREAD filling on the underside of half of the slices. Cover with remaining slices.

Honey-Almond Tartlets

Recipe No. 602

Dough:

410 g	all-purpose flour	3 cups
1 mL	**oetker** baking powder	¼ tsp
150 g	icing sugar, sifted	1⅓ cups
1 pkg	**oetker** vanilla sugar	1 pkg
2 drops	**oetker** lemon flavouring concentrate	2 drops
1	egg	1
1	egg yolk	1
280 g	butter or margarine, cold	1¼ cups

Filling:

250 g	sugar	1 cup
225 g	butter	1 cup
125 mL	honey	½ cup
500 g	almonds, sliced	3¾ cups
1 pkg	**oetker** vanilla sugar	1 pkg

MIX together flour and baking powder.
SIFT onto a working surface.
MAKE a well in the centre. Put icing sugar, vanilla sugar, flavouring, egg and egg yolk in the well.
COVER with flour and work into a thick paste.
CUT the cold butter or margarine in small pieces over the flour mixture.
STARTING from the centre, work all ingredients into a smooth dough.
CHILL for one-half hour.
PREHEAT oven to 190°C (375°F).
ON a lightly floured surface, roll out dough thinly.
USING a round cookie cutter, cut out slices.
LINE small muffin tins with dough.
BAKE for 10-12 minutes.

Filling:

IN a saucepan, combine sugar, butter and honey. Heat until sugar has completely dissolved.
STIR in almonds and vanilla sugar.
COOL slightly.
SPOON warm filling into shells.
BAKE for an additional 6-8 minutes.

Chocolate Dreams

Recipe No. 603

Ingredients:

125 g	semi-sweet chocolate, softened	4¹/₂ squares
255 g	marzipan	9 oz
90 g	icing sugar, sifted	³/₄ cup
1 pkg	**oetker** vanilla sugar	1 pkg
2	egg whites	2
1 mL	cinnamon	¹/₄ tsp

Cream Filling:

125 mL	whipping cream	¹/₂ cup
150 g	white chocolate, chopped	5¹/₂ squares
some	Grand Marnier	some

Decoration:

| some | butter cream filling chocolate curls* | some |

LIGHTLY grease a baking sheet.
IN a mixing bowl, combine chocolate, marzipan, icing sugar, vanilla sugar, egg whites and cinnamon. Work all ingredients into a smooth dough.
CHILL for one-half hour.
ROLL out dough 3 mm (¹/₈") thick.
USING a small round cookie cutter, cut out slices.
PLACE on prepared baking sheet.
LET rest for one-half hour.
PREHEAT oven to 190°C (375°F).
BAKE for 18 minutes.

Cream Filling:

IN a saucepan, combine whipping cream and white chocolate.
STIRRING constantly, heat mixture over medium heat until chocolate has melted.
POUR chocolate mixture into a mixing bowl.
CHILL.
ADD Grand Marnier.
BEAT mixture with an electric mixer until well blended.
SPREAD filling on the underside of half of the slices. Cover with remaining slices.
DECORATE with butter cream filling and chocolate curls.

*Chocolate Curls:

USE a bar of sweet chocolate at room temperature to make curls. Using a vegetable peeler, shave thin slices from the flat surface of the chocolate bar. The chocolate will curl as you shave.

Orange Magic

Recipe No. 604

Ingredients:

180 g	butter or margarine, softened	³/₄ cup	
200 g	icing sugar, sifted	1³/₄ cups	
4 drops	**oetker** orange flavouring concentrate	4 drops	
100 g	all-purpose flour	³/₄ cup	
250 g	candied orange peel, finely chopped	1¹/₂ cups	
250 g	almonds, coarsely chopped	2 cups	
50 mL	cold milk	¹/₄ cup	

Filling:

some	orange marmalade	some	

Glaze:

1 pkg	**oetker** Chocofix	1 pkg	

PREHEAT oven to 190°C-200°C (375°F-400°F).
IN a mixing bowl, combine butter or margarine, icing sugar and flavouring.
BEAT until fluffy.
MIX together flour, orange peel and almonds.
STIR alternately with the milk into the butter mixture.
DROP from a teaspoon 5 cm (2") apart onto baking sheet.
BAKE for 5-7 minutes.
REMOVE cookies from baking sheet.
COOL completely.

Filling:
SPREAD marmalade on the underside of half of the cookies. Cover with remaining cookies.

Glaze:
PREPARE Chocofix according to package directions.
DIP cookies into glaze.

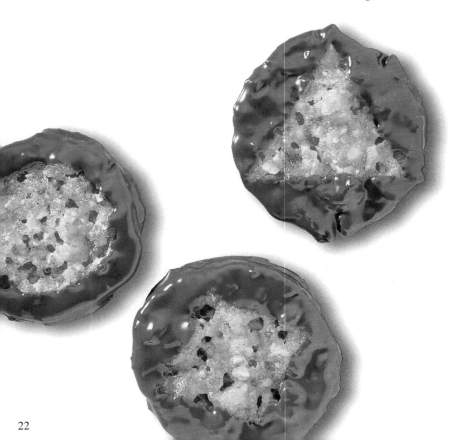

*A*nisettes

Recipe No. 605

Ingredients:

230 g	butter or margarine, softened	1 cup
225 g	icing sugar, sifted	2 cups
1 pkg	**oetker** vanilla sugar	1 pkg
1	egg	1
1	egg yolk	1
¹/₂ btl	**oetker** lemon flavouring concentrate	¹/₂ btl
350 g	all-purpose flour	2¹/₂ cups
50 g	**oetker** Gustin corn starch	¹/₃ cup
pinch	salt	pinch

Sprinkling:

some	aniseed	some

PREHEAT oven to 190°C (375°F).
IN a mixing bowl, combine butter or margarine, icing sugar, vanilla sugar, egg, egg yolk and flavouring.
BEAT until fluffy.
MIX together flour, corn starch and salt.
SIFT over butter mixture.
FOLD in gently but thoroughly.
DROP from a teaspoon onto baking sheet.
SHAPE.
SPRINKLE some aniseed on each biscuit.
BAKE for 8-10 minutes.

Walnut Treats

Recipe No. 606

Dough:

300 g	all-purpose flour	2¹/₄	cups
120 g	icing sugar, sifted	1	cup
1 pkg	**oetker** vanilla sugar	1	pkg
60 g	walnuts, ground	²/₃	cup
1	egg yolk	1	
210 g	butter or margarine, cold	1	cup

Filling:

some	fruit jam		some

Topping:

200 g	marzipan	7	oz
50 g	icing sugar, sifted	¹/₂	cup

Glaze:

250 g	icing sugar	2¹/₂	cups
15 mL	lemon juice	1	tbsp
30 mL	water	2	tbsp

Decoration:

some	walnut halves		some

PREHEAT oven to 190°C (375°F).
SIFT flour onto a working surface.
MAKE a well in the centre. Put icing sugar, vanilla sugar, walnuts and egg yolk in the well.
CUT cold butter or margarine in small pieces over the ingredients in the well.
STARTING from the centre, work all ingredients into a smooth dough.
ROLL out dough 3 mm (¹/₈") thick.
USING a round cookie cutter with scalloped edges, cut out slices 5 cm (2") in diameter.
PLACE on baking sheet.
BAKE for 10-12 minutes. Cool one minute before removing to wire rack.
COOL completely.

Topping:
COMBINE marzipan and icing sugar. Knead well.
ROLL out marzipan mixture thinly.
USING a round cookie cutter with scalloped edges, cut out slices 5 cm (2") in diameter.
BRUSH the underside of half of the baked slices with jam. Cover with remaining slices.
TOP with marzipan slices.

Glaze:
SIFT icing sugar into a mixing bowl.
ADD lemon juice and water.
BLEND until mixture is of a thick consistency.
SPREAD glaze on cookies.
DECORATE with walnut halves.

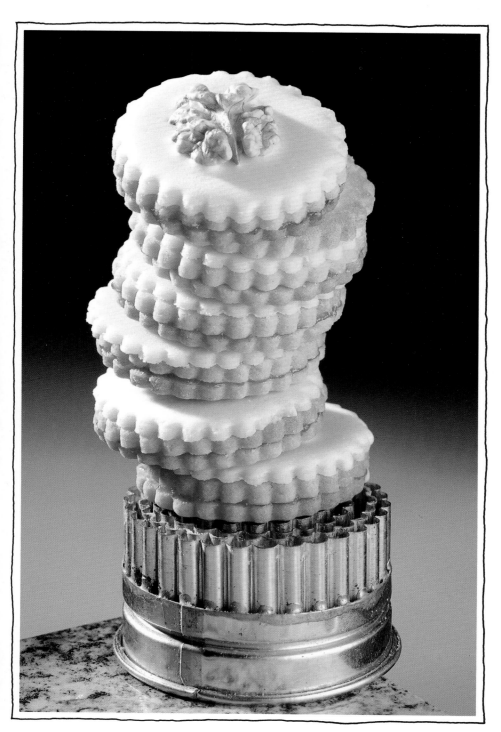

Almond Boughs

Recipe No. 607

Ingredients:

4	egg whites	4	
.5 mL	cream of tartar	1/8	tsp
210 g	sugar	1	cup
1 pkg	**oetker** vanilla sugar	1	pkg
1 mL	cinnamon	1/4	tsp
170 g	almonds, sliced	1 1/4	cups
3	square baking wafers	3	

BEAT egg whites until frothy. Sift cream of tartar over surface, continue beating.
GRADUALLY beat in sugar, vanilla sugar and cinnamon.
CONTINUE beating until mass is stiff.
FOLD in almonds gently but thoroughly.
SPREAD mixture on baking wafers.
LET rest in the refrigerator for one-half hour.
CUT into strips.
PREHEAT oven to 120°C (250°F). Sprinkle the outside of a tube form with flour.
PLACE dough strips over prepared tube form.
PLACE tube form on a baking sheet.
BAKE for 40-60 minutes.
COOL completely before removing boughs.

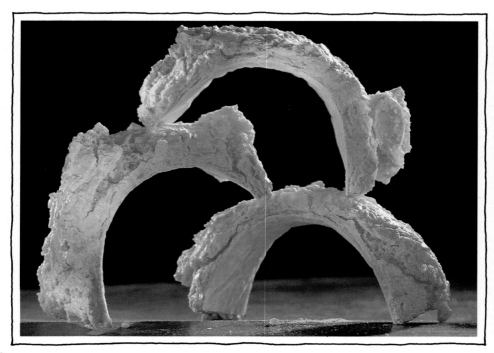

Easy Hazelnut Cookies

Recipe No. 608

Dough:

300 g	all-purpose flour	2¼	cups
1 mL	**oetker** baking powder	¼	tsp
120 g	icing sugar, sifted	1	cup
1 pkg	**oetker** vanilla sugar	1	pkg
½ btl	**oetker** lemon flavouring concentrate	½	btl
60 g	hazelnuts, ground	⅔	cup
3	egg yolks	3	
230 g	butter or margarine, cold	1	cup

Brushing:

1	egg, whisked	1	

Sprinkling:

100 g	almonds, sliced	¾	cup

Filling:

some	red currant jam	some	

MIX together flour and baking powder.
SIFT onto a working surface.
MAKE a well in the centre. Put icing sugar, vanilla sugar, flavouring, hazelnuts and egg yolks in the well.
CUT butter or margarine in small pieces over the ingredients in the well.
COVER with flour.
STARTING from the centre, work all ingredients into a smooth dough.
CHILL for one-half hour.
PREHEAT oven to 190°C (375°F).
SHAPE dough into 2.5 cm (1") balls.
PLACE on baking sheet. Press down centres with thumb.
BRUSH balls with egg.
SPRINKLE with almond slices.
FILL centres with jam.
BAKE for 10-12 minutes.

Orange Macaroons

Recipe No. 609

Ingredients:

125 g	walnuts, ground	1¹/₃	cups
240 g	icing sugar, sifted	2¹/₄	cups
3	egg whites	3	
1 pkg	**oetker** vanilla sugar	1	pkg
1 mL	cinnamon	¹/₄	tsp
pinch	salt		pinch
5 drops	**oetker** lemon flavouring concentrate	5	drops
50 g	candied orange peel, diced	¹/₄	cup

Cream Filling:

125 mL	whipping cream	¹/₂	cup
125 g	semi-sweet chocolate, chopped	4	squares
15 mL	orange liqueur	1	tbsp

Brushing:

30 mL	orange jam, heated	2	tbsp

Glaze:

1 pkg	**oetker** Chocofix	1	pkg

Decoration:

orange zest, (finely sliced orange peel)

PREHEAT oven to 120°C (250°F). Lightly grease a baking sheet.
IN a mixing bowl, combine walnuts, icing sugar, egg whites, vanilla sugar, cinnamon, salt, flavouring and candied orange peel.
PLACE bowl in a water bath and heat to 35-40°C (100°F). Stir constantly.
CHILL mixture.
PUT mixture in a pastry bag fitted with a round tube.
PIPE walnut size portions onto prepared baking sheet.
BAKE for 40-50 minutes.

Cream Filling:

IN a saucepan, combine whipping cream and chocolate.
STIRRING constantly, heat mixture over medium heat until chocolate has melted.
POUR mixture into a bowl. Chill.
ADD orange liqueur to chilled mixture.
USING an electric mixer, beat until blended.
SPREAD the underside of half of the macaroons with cream. Cover with remaining macaroons.
BRUSH tops with heated jam.

Glaze:

PREPARE Chocofix according to package directions.
DIP the underside of each cookie into the glaze.
PLACE cookies on waxed paper. Let set.
DRIZZLE tops with chocolate glaze or decorate with orange peel.

Cherry Squares

Recipe No. 610

Dough:

75 g	butter or margarine, softened	$^1/_3$ cup
75 g	icing sugar, sifted	$^2/_3$ cup
1 pkg	**oetker** vanilla sugar	1 pkg
2	egg yolks	2
200 g	all-purpose flour	$1^1/_2$ cups

Topping:

200 mL	cherry jam	$^3/_4$ cup
some	kirsch (cherry brandy)	some
30 mL	sugar	2 tbsp
200 g	marzipan	7 oz
100 g	icing sugar, sifted	$^3/_4$ cup

Brushing:

1	egg white, beaten	1

Glaze:

100 g	icing sugar, sifted	$^3/_4$ cup
15 mL	cherry juice	1 tbsp
15-30 mL	hot water	1-2 tbsp

LIGHTLY grease a 23 x 23 cm (9 x 9") cake pan.
IN a mixing bowl, combine butter or margarine, icing sugar, vanilla sugar and egg yolks.
BEAT until fluffy.
SIFT flour over butter mixture. Quickly but carefully, knead into butter mixture.
CHILL for one-half hour.
PREHEAT oven to 180°C (350°F).
ROLL out dough. Press evenly into bottom of prepared pan.
BAKE for 10-12 minutes.

Topping:
IN a saucepan, combine jam, kirsch and sugar.
HEAT for 2 minutes.
IN a mixing bowl, combine marzipan and icing sugar. Knead well.
ROLL out marzipan mixture into a square measuring 23 x 23 cm (9 x 9").
SPREAD jam on baked square.
TOP with marzipan square.
LIGHTLY brush marzipan surface with egg white.
BAKE for 5 minutes.
SLICE warm pastry into 3 x 3 cm ($1^1/_4$ x $1^1/_4$") squares.

Glaze:
IN a mixing bowl, combine icing sugar and cherry juice. Add water until mixture is of a thick consistency.
GLAZE each square.
CHILL until glaze has set.

*A*lmond Linzer Cookies

Recipe No. 611

Dough:

320 g	all-purpose flour	2¹/₃ cups	
pinch	salt	pinch	
1 mL	cinnamon	¹/₄ tsp	
100 g	icing sugar, sifted	³/₄ cup	
1 pkg	**oetker** vanilla sugar	1 pkg	
100 g	almonds, ground	1 cup	
¹/₂ btl	**oetker** almond flavouring concentrate	¹/₂ btl	
2	egg yolks	2	
180 g	butter or margarine, cold	³/₄ cup	

Filling:

200 mL	orange marmalade	³/₄ cup

Dusting:

some	icing sugar, sifted	some

SIFT flour onto a working surface.
MAKE a well in the centre. Put salt, cinnamon, icing sugar, vanilla sugar, almonds, flavouring and egg yolks in the well.
CUT butter or margarine in small pieces over the ingredients in the well.
COVER with flour
STARTING from the centre, work all ingredients into a smooth dough.
CHILL for one-half hour.
PREHEAT oven to 180°C (350°F).
ROLL out dough thinly.
USING a round cookie cutter with scalloped edges, cut out slices 5 cm (2") in diameter.
TO one-half of the slices, cut out three holes in each slice.
PLACE all slices on baking sheet.
BAKE for 10-12 minutes.
REMOVE from baking sheet.
SPREAD the underside of all the slices without holes with marmalade. Top with slices with holes.
DUST tops with icing sugar.

*L*emon Crescents

Recipe No. 612

Dough:

300 g	all-purpose flour	2¹/₄ cups	
80 g	pecans, ground	³/₄ cup	
80 g	icing sugar, sifted	³/₄ cup	
1 pkg	**oetker** vanilla sugar	1 pkg	
¹/₂ btl	**oetker** lemon flavouring concentrate	¹/₂ btl	
	pinch salt	pinch	
220 g	butter or margarine, cold	1 cup	

Dusting:

120 g	icing sugar, sifted	1 cup	
1 pkg	**oetker** vanilla sugar	1 pkg	

PREHEAT oven to 180°C (350°F).

SIFT flour onto a working surface.

MAKE a well in the centre. Put pecans, icing sugar, vanilla sugar, flavouring and salt in the well.

CUT butter or margarine in small pieces over the ingredients in the well.

COVER with flour.

STARTING at the centre, work all ingredients into a smooth dough.

SHAPE dough into rolls the size of a pencil.

CUT into 5 cm (2") long pieces.

SHAPE into crescents. Place on baking sheet.

BAKE for 12 minutes.

Dusting:

MIX together icing sugar and vanilla sugar.

ROLL crescents in sugar mixture while hot.

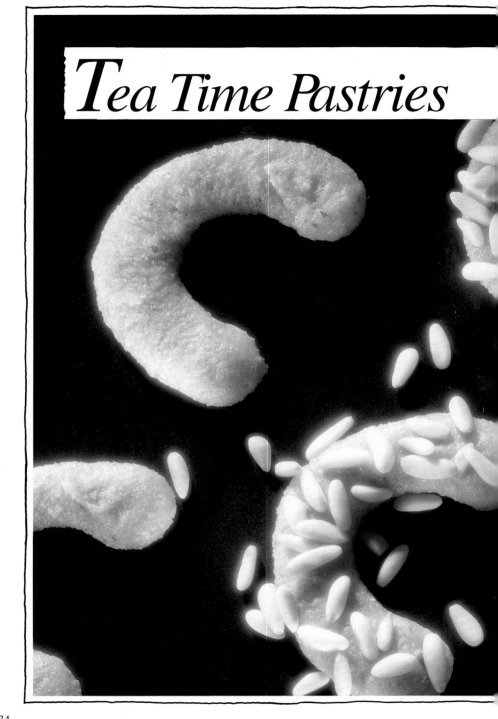

Tea Time Pastries

Florentine Slices

Recipe No. 613

Dough:

350 g	all-purpose flour	2¹/₂	cups
5 mL	**oetker** baking powder	1	tsp
pinch	salt		pinch
120 g	icing sugar, sifted	1	cup
1 pkg	**oetker** vanilla sugar	1	pkg
1	egg	1	
3 drops	**oetker** lemon flavouring concentrate	3	drops
225 g	butter or margarine, cold	1	cup

Topping:

200 g	sugar	1	cup
250 mL	whipping cream	1	cup
120 mL	honey	¹/₂	cup
110 g	butter	¹/₂	cup
310 g	almonds, sliced	3¹/₂	cups
100 g	candied orange peel, chopped	²/₃	cup

Brushing:

30 mL	red currant jam	2	tbsp

Glaze:

1-2 pkgs	**oetker** Chocofix	1-2	pkgs

LINE two baking sheets with parchment paper.
MIX together flour and baking powder.
SIFT onto a working surface.
MAKE a well in the centre, put salt, icing sugar, vanilla sugar, egg and flavouring in the well.
CUT butter or margarine in small pieces over the ingredients in the well.
COVER with flour.
STARTING from the centre, work all ingredients into a smooth dough.
CHILL for one-half hour.
PREHEAT oven to 175°C (350°F).
DIVIDE dough into two equal parts.
ROLL out each part to measure 25 x 30 cm (10 x 12").
PRICK dough with a fork several times.
PLACE dough on prepared baking sheets.
BAKE for 12-15 minutes.
REMOVE from baking sheets.

Topping:
IN a saucepan, combine sugar, whipping cream, honey and butter.
COOK until mixture is golden yellow.
STIR in almonds and candied peel.
LET cool.
SPREAD almond mixture evenly over one layer of cake.
PLACE on baking sheet.
BAKE for an additional 10-12 minutes.
REMOVE from baking sheet.
COOL completely.

Brushing:
SPREAD second layer of cake with red currant jam.
TOP with almond covered layer.
CUT into slices.

Glaze:
PREPARE Chocofix according to package directions.
BRUSH chocolate evenly on the sides of each slice.

*O*range Hearts

Recipe No. 614

Ingredients:

4	egg whites	4	
.5 mL	cream of tartar	1/8	tsp
250 g	sugar	1	cup
1 mL	salt	1/4	tsp
4 drops	**oetker** orange flavouring concentrate	4	drops
125 g	walnuts or almonds, ground	1 1/3	cups

Brushing:

45 mL	orange marmalade, heated	3	tbsp

Glaze:

1 pkg	**oetker** Chocofix	1	pkg

PREHEAT oven to 120°C (250°F). Lightly grease a baking sheet.

BEAT egg whites until frothy. Sift cream of tartar over surface, continue beating.

GRADUALLY beat in sugar. Continue beating until mass is stiff.

BEAT in salt and flavouring. Fold in nuts.

PLACE mixture in pastry bag fitted with a round tube.

PIPE heart shapes onto prepared baking sheet.

BAKE for 40-60 minutes.

REMOVE hearts from baking sheet.

BRUSH with marmalade. Cool completely.

PREPARE Chocofix according to package directions.

GLAZE hearts.

Sultana Biscuits

Recipe No. 615

Batter:

225 g	butter, softened	1	cup
250 g	icing sugar, sifted	2¼	cups
1 pkg	**oetker** vanilla sugar	1	pkg
2	eggs	2	
250 g	all-purpose flour	1¾	cups
1 mL	**oetker** baking powder	¼	tsp
60 g	raisins, finely chopped	⅓	cup

Brushing:

some	red currant jam		some

Dipping:

1 pkg	**oetker** Chocofix	1	pkg

PREHEAT oven to 170°C (350°F).
IN a mixing bowl, combine butter, icing sugar and vanilla sugar.
BEAT until fluffy.
ADD eggs, one at a time.
MIX together flour and baking powder.
SIFT over butter mixture.
FOLD in raisins, one tablespoon at a time.
PLACE mixture in a pastry bag fitted with a large round tube.
PIPE 5 cm (2") long bars, the thickness of a finger, onto baking sheet.
BAKE for 10-12 minutes.
COOL completely.
REMOVE biscuits from baking sheet.
BRUSH jam on the underside of half of the biscuits. Cover with remaining biscuits.
PREPARE Chocofix according to package directions.
DIP biscuits in chocolate.

*H*azelnut Half-Moons

Recipe No. 616

Dough:

350 g	all-purpose flour	2¹/₂ cups
1 mL	**oetker** baking powder	¹/₄ tsp
pinch	salt	pinch
120 g	icing sugar, sifted	1 cup
1 pkg	**oetker** vanilla sugar	1 pkg
1	egg	1
1	egg yolk	1
220 g	butter or margarine, cold	1 cup

Brushing:

1	egg white, beaten	1

Cream Filling:

150 g	milk chocolate	6 squares
125 mL	whipping cream	¹/₂ cup
¹/₂ btl	**oetker** rum flavouring concentrate	¹/₂ btl

Topping:

60 g	hazelnuts, toasted, coarsely chopped	¹/₂ cup

Glaze:

2 pkgs	**oetker** Chocofix	2 pkgs

MIX together flour and baking powder.
SIFT onto a working surface.
MAKE a well in the centre. Put salt, icing sugar, vanilla sugar, egg and egg yolk in the well.
CUT butter or margarine in small pieces over the ingredients in the well.
STARTING from the centre, work all ingredients into a smooth dough.
CHILL for one hour.
PREHEAT oven to 190°C (375°F).
ROLL out dough 3 mm (¹/₈") thick.
USING a moon or crescent shaped cookie cutter, cut out shapes.
PLACE shapes on baking sheet.
LIGHTLY brush each cookie with beaten egg white.
BAKE for 10-12 minutes.

Cream Filling:

BREAK chocolate into small pieces and place in a saucepan.
ADD whipping cream.
STIRRING constantly over medium heat, heat until chocolate has melted.
POUR mixture into a mixing bowl.
STIR in flavouring. Chill.
USING an electric mixer, beat chilled cream for 2-3 minutes.
SPREAD cream over surface of cookies.
TOP with hazelnuts.
CHILL for one-half hour.

Glaze:

PREPARE Chocofix according to package directions.
GLAZE biscuits.

Train Tracks

Recipe No. 617

Dough:

300	g	all-purpose flour	2¼	cups
1	mL	**oetker** baking powder	¼	tsp
	pinch	salt		pinch
100	g	icing sugar, sifted	¾	cup
1	pkg	**oetker** vanilla sugar	1	pkg
1		egg	1	
2	drops	**oetker** lemon flavouring concentrate	2	drops
220	g	butter or margarine, cold	1	cup

Macaroon Mixture:

4		egg whites	4	
.5	mL	cream of tartar	⅛	tsp
200	g	sugar	1	cup
1	mL	cloves, ground	¼	tsp
1	mL	cinnamon	¼	tsp
125	g	walnuts, ground	1⅓	cups

Filling:

75	mL	red currant jam, heated	⅓	cup

LIGHTLY grease a baking sheet.
MIX together flour and baking powder.
SIFT onto a working surface.
MAKE a well in the centre. Put salt, icing sugar, vanilla sugar, egg and flavouring in the well.
CUT butter or margarine in small pieces over the ingredients in the well.
STARTING from the centre, work all ingredients into a smooth dough.
CHILL for one-half hour.
PREHEAT oven to 160°C (325°F).
ROLL out dough 3 mm (⅛") thick.
CUT into 5 cm (2") wide strips.
PLACE strips on prepared baking sheet.

Macaroon Mixture:

BEAT egg whites until frothy. Sift cream of tartar over surface, continue beating.
GRADUALLY beat in sugar. Continue beating until mass is stiff.
BEAT in spices. Fold in walnuts
PLACE mixture in a pastry bag fitted with a small round tube.
PIPE three strips of macaroon mixture on each strip of dough.
BAKE for 20 minutes.
COOL completely.
FILL grooves with jam (see photo).

Marzipan Macaroons

Recipe No. 618

Ingredients:

250 g	marzipan	9	oz
220 g	icing sugar, sifted	2	cups
3	egg whites	3	
1 pkg	**oetker** vanilla sugar	1	pkg

Filling:

75 mL	red currant jam, heated	⅓	cup

Dipping:

1 pkg	**oetker** Chocofix	1	pkg

Decoration:

walnut halves

PREHEAT oven to 120°C (250°F). Grease a baking sheet.
IN a mixing bowl, combine marzipan, icing sugar, egg whites and vanilla sugar.
BEAT until marzipan mixture is lump-free.
PLACE mixture in a pastry bag fitted with a round tube.
PIPE walnut size portions onto prepared baking sheet.
BAKE for 40 minutes.
COOL completely.

Filling:
REMOVE cookies from baking sheet.
SPREAD jam 3 mm (⅛″) thick on the underside of each cookie.

Dipping:
PREPARE Chocofix according to package directions.
DIP the underside (side with jam) of the cookies in chocolate.
LET set.
TOP with walnut halves. Fasten with a drop of Chocofix.

*P*ine Nut Crescents

Recipe No. 619

Ingredients:

4	egg whites	4	
.5 mL	cream of tartar	1/8	tsp
200 g	sugar	1	cup
1 mL	cinnamon	1/4	tsp
1 mL	cloves, powdered	1/4	tsp
2 drops	**oetker** lemon flavouring concentrate	2	drops
125 g	hazelnuts, ground	1 1/3	cups

Sprinkling:

55 g	pine nuts	1/3	cup

PREHEAT oven to 120°C (250°F). Grease a baking sheet.

BEAT egg whites until frothy. Sift cream of tartar over surface, continue beating.

GRADUALLY beat in sugar. Continue beating until mass is stiff.

BEAT in spices and flavouring. Fold in hazelnuts.

PLACE mixture in a pastry bag fitted with a round tube.

PIPE crescents, 8 cm (3") in length, onto prepared baking sheet.

SPRINKLE with pine nuts.

BAKE for 40-60 minutes.

*W*alnut Darlings

Recipe No. 620

Ingredients:

4	egg whites	4	
.5 mL	cream of tartar	$^1/_8$	tsp
50 g	sugar	$^1/_4$	cup
90 g	icing sugar, sifted	$^3/_4$	cup
1 pkg	**oetker** vanilla sugar	1	pkg
60 g	walnuts, ground	$^2/_3$	cup

Cream Filling:

150 g	milk chocolate	5	squares
125 mL	whipping cream	$^1/_2$	cup
$^1/_2$ btl	**oetker** rum flavouring concentrate	$^1/_2$	btl

Glaze:

1 pkg	**oetker** Chocofix	1	pkg

Topping:

walnut halves

PREHEAT oven to 120°C (250°F). Lightly grease a baking sheet.
BEAT egg whites until frothy.
SIFT cream of tartar over surface, continue beating.
GRADUALLY beat in sugar, icing sugar and vanilla sugar. Continue beating until mass is stiff.
FOLD in walnuts, gently but thoroughly.
DROP on baking sheet.
BAKE for 40-60 minutes.

Cream Filling:

BREAK chocolate into small pieces and place in saucepan.
ADD whipping cream.
STIRRING constantly over medium heat, heat mixture until chocolate has melted.
POUR mixture into a mixing bowl.
STIR in flavouring. Chill.
USING an electric mixer, beat chilled cream for 2-3 minutes.
RESERVE some of the cream for decoration.
SPREAD cream on the underside of half of the cookies. Cover with remaining cookies.
PLACE a dab of the reserved cream in the centre of each cookie.

Glaze:

PREPARE Chocofix according to package directions.
GLAZE surface of each cookie.
TOP with walnut halves.

47

Almond Buttons

Recipe No. 621

Dough:

3	eggs	3	
200 g	icing sugar, sifted	2	cups
1 pkg	**oetker** vanilla sugar	1	pkg
5 drops	**oetker** lemon flavouring concentrate	5	drops
125 g	almonds, ground	1¼	cups
125 g	vanilla wafer crumbs	1¼	cups
150 g	all-purpose flour	1¼	cups

LIGHTLY grease a baking sheet.
IN a mixing bowl, combine eggs, icing sugar, vanilla sugar and flavouring.
BEAT until fluffy.
GENTLY but thoroughly fold in almonds, vanilla wafer crumbs and flour.
LET rest for twenty minutes.
PREHEAT oven to 190°C (375°F).
SHAPE dough into rolls the size of a finger.
SLICE each roll into 3 cm (1¼") long pieces.
SHAPE each piece into a ball. Flatten slightly.
PLACE balls on prepared baking sheet.
USING a knife, make a cross on the surface of each biscuit.
BAKE for 10 minutes.

Coffee Rounds

Recipe No. 622

Ingredients:

225 g	butter, softened	1	cup
425 g	sugar	2	cups
1 pkg	**oetker** vanilla sugar	1	pkg
2	eggs	2	
500 g	all-purpose flour	3½	cups
1 pkg	**oetker** baking powder	1	pkg
15 mL	instant coffee, dissolved in some hot water	1	tbsp
115 g	currants	¾	cup

Brushing:

1	egg, beaten	1	

Sprinkling:

sugar crystals

PREHEAT oven to 180°C (350°F).
IN a mixing bowl, combine butter, sugar, vanilla sugar and eggs.
BEAT until fluffy.
MIX together flour and baking powder.
SIFT over butter mixture. Mix well.
QUICKLY but thoroughly fold in dissolved instant coffee and currants.
PLACE mixture in a pastry bag fitted with a large round tube.
PIPE walnut size portions onto baking sheet.
BRUSH lightly with beaten egg.
SPRINKLE with sugar crystals.
BAKE for 10-12 minutes.

49

*M*arzipan Boats

Recipe No. 623

Dough:

200	g	all-purpose flour	1¹/₂	cups
1	mL	**oetker** baking powder	¹/₄	tsp
70	g	icing sugar, sifted	¹/₂	cup
¹/₂	pkg	**oetker** vanilla sugar	¹/₂	pkg
	pinch	salt		pinch
1		egg	1	
110	g	butter or margarine, cold	¹/₂	cup

Filling:

120	g	marzipan	4¹/₂	oz
3		egg yolks	3	
1	mL	cinnamon	¹/₄	tsp
2	drops	**oetker** lemon flavouring concentrate	2	drops
15	mL	Grand Marnier	1	tbsp

Brushing:

30	mL	raspberry jam, heated	2	tbsp

MIX together flour and baking powder.
SIFT onto a working surface.
MAKE a well in the centre. Put icing sugar, vanilla sugar, salt and egg in the well.
CUT butter or margarine in small pieces over the ingredients in the well.
COVER with flour.
STARTING at the centre, work all ingredients into a smooth dough.
CHILL for one-half hour.
PREHEAT oven to 180°C (350°F).
ROLL out dough 3 mm (¹/₈") thick.
USING a knife, cut dough. Line small boat-shaped pans.
(**HINT**: Place boat shaped pans close together. Lay dough loosely over pans. Press lightly. Using a rolling pin, roll over dough on pans.)

Filling:

IN a mixing bowl, combine marzipan, egg yolks, cinnamon, flavouring and Grand Marnier.
BEAT until mixture is of a smooth consistency.
PLACE mixture in a pastry bag fitted with a small round tube.
PIPE filling in a spiral fashion into the dough-lined pans.
PLACE pans on baking sheet.
BAKE for 12-15 minutes.
COOL completely.
REMOVE from pans. Brush with warm jam.

Chocolate Bells

Recipe No. 624

Ingredients:

4	egg whites	4	
.5 mL	cream of tartar	¹/₈ tsp	
50 g	sugar	¹/₄ cup	
90 g	icing sugar, sifted	³/₄ cup	
4 drops	**oetker** vanilla flavouring concentrate	4 drops	
60 g	almonds, toasted, ground	²/₃ cup	

Cream Filling:

150 g	milk chocolate	6 squares	
125 mL	whipping cream	¹/₂ cup	
5 mL	instant coffee	1 tsp	

Glaze:

1 pkg	**oetker** Chocofix	1 pkg	

Topping:

gold or silver sugar pearls

PREHEAT oven to 120°C (250°F). Lightly grease a baking sheet.
BEAT egg whites until frothy. Sift cream of tartar over surface, continue beating.
GRADUALLY beat in sugar and icing sugar.
CONTINUE beating until mass is stiff.
BEAT in flavouring. Fold in almonds gently but thoroughly.
PLACE mixture in a pastry bag fitted with a round tube.
PIPE rounds, 5 cm (2") in diameter, onto prepared baking sheet.
BAKE for 40-60 minutes.

Cream Filling:

BREAK chocolate into small pieces and place in a saucepan. Add whipping cream and instant coffee.
STIRRING constantly over medium heat, heat mixture until the chocolate has melted.
POUR mixture into a mixing bowl. Chill.
USING an electric mixer, beat chilled cream for 2-3 minutes.
SPOON cream onto cookies. Shape into small domes.

Glaze:

PREPARE Chocofix according to package directions.
GLAZE domes with chocolate.
DECORATE with gold or silver sugar pearls.

Sweet Kisses

Recipe No. 625

Ingredients:

250	mL	whipping cream	1	cup
80	g	sugar	$^1/_3$	cup
1	pkg	**oetker** vanilla sugar	1	pkg
5		egg whites	5	
75	g	icing sugar, sifted	$^2/_3$	cup
235	g	all-purpose flour	$1^3/_4$	cups

Cream Filling:

250	g	white chocolate	9	squares
125	mL	whipping cream	$^1/_2$	cup
30	mL	Curaçao liqueur	2	tbsp

Decoration:

red currant jam, heated

PREHEAT oven to 200°C (400°F). Lightly grease a baking sheet.

IN a mixing bowl, combine whipping cream, sugar and vanilla sugar.

BEAT until mixture is of a thick consistency.

IN another bowl, beat egg whites to stiff peaks.

GRADUALLY add icing sugar, while beating.

ADD whipping cream mixture to egg white mixture.

SIFT flour over top. Fold in gently but thoroughly.

PLACE mixture in a pastry bag fitted with a small round tube.

PIPE hazelnut size portions, well apart, onto prepared baking sheet.

BAKE for 12 minutes.

REMOVE cookies from baking sheet while warm.

Cream Filling:

BREAK white chocolate into small pieces and place in a saucepan.

ADD whipping cream.

STIRRING constantly over medium heat, heat mixture until chocolate has melted.

POUR mixture into a bowl. Chill.

ADD liqueur.

USING an electric mixer, beat chilled cream until well blended.

SPREAD cream on the underside of half of the cookies. Cover with remaining cookies.

Decoration:

PLACE jam in a pastry bag.

DECORATE surface of cookies, as desired.

55

Festive Treats

Gingerbread Delights

Recipe No. 626

Dough:

500	mL	honey	2 cups
125	mL	water	¹/₂ cup
200	g	sugar	1 cup
2	pkgs	**oetker** vanilla sugar	2 pkgs
		juice and peel of 1 lemon	
		juice and peel of 1 orange	
500	g	whole wheat flour	4 cups
575	g	rye flour	5 cups
1	pkg	**oetker** baking powder	1 pkg
5	mL	baking soda	1 tsp
90	mL	cinnamon	6 tbsp
30	mL	cloves, ground	2 tbsp
15	mL	nutmeg	1 tbsp
30	mL	ginger	2 tbsp
45	mL	coriander	3 tbsp
4		eggs	4

Glaze:

120	g	icing sugar	1 cup
15-			
30	mL	water	1-2 tbsp
	pinch	salt	pinch
3	drops	lemon juice	3 drops
		food colouring	

Topping:

candied fruit, sugar sprinkles, etc.

IN a saucepan, combine honey, water, sugar, vanilla sugar, lemon juice, orange juice, lemon and orange peel.
BRING to a boil while stirring constantly.
POUR mixture into a mixing bowl. Cool slightly.
MIX together flours, baking powder, baking soda and spices.
ADD flour mixture to honey mixture.
WORK all ingredients into a smooth dough.
COVER and chill for two to three days.
PREHEAT oven to 180°C (350°F).
KNEAD eggs into the dough.
ROLL dough ¹/₂ cm (⁵/₈") thick.
USING a variety of cookie cutters, cut out shapes.
PLACE shapes on prepared baking sheet.
BAKE for 10 minutes.

Glaze:
SIFT icing sugar into a mixing bowl.
ADD water, salt and lemon juice.
BEAT until mixture is of a thick consistency.
PORTION out mixture. Add a different food colour to each portion.
DECORATE gingerbread as desired.
TOP with candied fruit, sugar sprinkles etc.

*W*ine Rosettes

Recipe No. 627

Ingredients:

225 g	butter, softened	1 cup	
250 g	icing sugar, sifted	2 cups	
1 pkg	**oetker** vanilla sugar	1 pkg	
pinch	nutmeg	pinch	
150 mL	red wine	²/₃ cup	
¹/₂ btl	**oetker** lemon flavouring concentrate	¹/₂ btl	
500 g	all-purpose flour	3¹/₂ cups	
5 mL	**oetker** baking powder	1 tsp	

PREHEAT oven to 190°C (375°F).
IN a mixing bowl, combine butter, icing sugar, vanilla sugar and nutmeg.
BEAT until fluffy.
GRADUALLY add wine and flavouring. Mix well.
MIX together flour and baking powder.
SIFT over butter mixture. Beat well.
PLACE mixture in a pastry bag fitted with a star tube.
PIPE small rosettes onto baking sheet.
BAKE for 8-10 minutes.

Chocolate Stars

Recipe No. 628

Dough:

100 g	marzipan	3¹/₂	oz
150 g	butter or margarine, cold	²/₃	cup
120 g	icing sugar, sifted	1	cup
2	eggs	2	
100 g	hazelnuts, ground	³/₄	cup
100 g	semi-sweet chocolate, melted	4	squares
50 mL	cold milk	¹/₄	cup
375 g	all-purpose flour	2²/₃	cups
1 pkg	**oetker** baking powder	1	pkg
pinch	salt		pinch

Glaze:

oetker Chocofix
pistachio nuts, halved

COMBINE *marzipan, butter or margarine, icing sugar and eggs. Work into a smooth dough.*
ADD *hazelnuts, chocolate and milk. Mix well.*
MIX *together flour, baking powder and salt.*
SIFT *one-half of the flour mixture over the marzipan mixture. Beat.*
KNEAD *remaining flour mixture into the marzipan mixture.*
CHILL *for 2 hours.*
PREHEAT *oven to 175°C (350°F).*
ROLL *dough 6 mm (¹/₄") thick.*
USING *round or star-shaped cookie cutters, cut out shapes. (See front cover.)*
PLACE *cookies on baking sheet.*
BAKE *for 10-12 minutes.*

Glaze:
PREPARE *Chocofix according to package directions.*
PLACE *a dab of glaze in the centre of each cookie.*
TOP *with pistachio nuts.*

61

*B*utter Rounds

Recipe No. 629

Dough:

220	g	butter, softened	1 cup
100	g	icing sugar, sifted	¾ cup
1	pkg	**oetker** vanilla sugar	1 pkg
135	g	all-purpose flour	1 cup
1	mL	salt	¼ tsp
200	g	**oetker** Gustin corn starch	2 cups

IN a mixing bowl, combine butter, icing sugar and vanilla sugar.
BEAT until fluffy.
MIX together flour, salt and corn starch.
SIFT one-half of the flour mixture over the butter mixture.
BEAT well.
KNEAD remaining flour mixture into the butter mixture.
CHILL for one-half hour.
PREHEAT oven to 180°C (350°F).
SHAPE dough into a roll.
USING a knife, cut dough into slices.
ROLL each slice into a ball.
PLACE balls on baking sheet.
PRESS down lightly on each cookie, using a fork.
BAKE for 12 minutes.

Chocolate Crescents

Recipe No. 630

Dough:

320 g	all-purpose flour	2¼	cups
5 mL	**oetker** baking powder	1	tsp
15 mL	cocoa	1	tbsp
120 g	icing sugar, sifted	1	cup
1 pkg	**oetker** vanilla sugar	1	pkg
75 g	semi-sweet chocolate, grated	3	squares
50 g	almonds, finely ground	½	cup
1	egg	1	
½ btl	**oetker** lemon flavouring concentrate	½	btl
220 g	butter or margarine, cold	1	cup

Glaze:

1 pkg	**oetker** Chocofix	1	pkg

Sprinkling:

some	chocolate, grated		some

MIX together flour, baking powder and cocoa.
SIFT onto a working surface.
MAKE a well in the centre. Put icing sugar, vanilla sugar, chocolate, almonds, egg and flavouring in the well.
CUT cold butter or margarine in small pieces over the ingredients in the well.
COVER with flour.
STARTING from the centre, work all ingredients into a smooth dough.
CHILL for one hour.
PREHEAT oven to 190°C (375°F).
SHAPE dough into rolls the size of a pencil.
CUT into 5 cm (2") long pieces.
SHAPE into crescents. Place on baking sheet.
BAKE for 12 minutes.
COOL completely.

Glaze:

PREPARE Chocofix according to package directions.
DIP the ends of each crescent into the glaze.
SPRINKLE grated chocolate over top of the glaze.

Macaroon Clouds

Recipe No. 631

Ingredients:

4	egg whites	4
200 g	sugar	1 cup
150 g	hazelnuts, ground	1½ cups
15 mL	all-purpose flour	2 tbsp
1 pkg	**oetker** vanilla sugar	1 pkg
100 g	hazelnuts, coarsely chopped	1 cup

Filling and Decorating:

some	raspberry jam	some

PREHEAT oven to 165°C (325°F). Lightly grease a baking sheet.

IN a mixing bowl, beat egg whites to very stiff peaks. (Peaks should be so stiff that when a knife is inserted, the cut remains visible.)

GRADUALLY add sugar. Continue beating until all the sugar has dissolved. (Approximately 15 minutes).

SPRINKLE ground nuts, flour and vanilla sugar over the mixture.

FOLD in gently but thoroughly.

PLACE mixture in a pastry bag fitted with a large round tube.

PIPE bars 5 cm (2") in length onto prepared baking sheet.

SPRINKLE with chopped hazelnuts.

BAKE for 18 minutes.

REMOVE bars from baking sheet while warm.

BRUSH jam on the underside of half of the bars. Top with remaining bars.

DRIZZLE jam on top of bars.

Honey Slices

Recipe No. 632

Dough:

460 g	all-purpose flour	3¹/₃	cups
5 mL	**oetker** baking powder	1	tsp
150 g	icing sugar, sifted	1¹/₃	cups
1 pkg	**oetker** vanilla sugar	1	pkg
¹/₂ btl	**oetker** lemon flavouring concentrate	¹/₂	btl
300 g	butter or margarine, cold	1¹/₂	cups

Filling:

30 mL	honey	2	tbsp

Sprinkling:

icing sugar, sifted

MIX together flour and baking powder.
SIFT onto a working surface.
MAKE a well in the centre. Put icing sugar, vanilla sugar and flavouring in the well.
CUT cold butter or margarine in small pieces over the ingredients in the well.
COVER with flour.
STARTING from the centre, work all ingredients into a smooth dough.
CHILL for one hour.
PREHEAT oven to 200°C (400°F).
ROLL out dough thinly.
USING a round cookie cutter, cut out slices 5 cm (2") in diameter.
PLACE slices on baking sheet.
BAKE for 6-8 minutes.
BRUSH the underside of half of the warm slices with honey. Top with remaining slices.
SPRINKLE with icing sugar.

Filled Gingerbread

Recipe No. 633

Dough:

250 mL	honey	1	cup
60 mL	water	$^1/_4$	cup
60 g	butter or margarine	$^1/_4$	cup
250 g	whole wheat flour	2	cups
250 g	rye flour	2	cups
	juice of 1 lemon		
1 pkg	**oetker** baking powder	1	pkg
5 mL	baking soda	1	tsp
5 mL	cinnamon	1	tsp
1 mL	ginger	$^1/_4$	tsp
1 mL	nutmeg	$^1/_4$	tsp
2 mL	cloves, ground	$^1/_2$	tsp
2	eggs	2	

Filling:

200 g	figs	1	cup
100 g	dates	$^1/_2$	cup
200 g	prunes	1	cup
100 g	raisins	$^3/_4$	cup
100 g	currants	$^2/_3$	cup
1 shot	rum	1	shot
200 g	walnuts, lightly toasted, chopped	2	cups
30 mL	orange marmalade	2	tbsp

Brushing:

15 mL	milk	2	tbsp

LINE a baking sheet with parchment paper.
IN a saucepan, combine honey and water.
BRING to a quick boil.
POUR into a mixing bowl. Cool slightly.
ADD butter or margarine, flours, lemon juice, baking powder, baking soda and spices.
KNEAD thoroughly.
CHILL overnight (preferably 2-3 days).
ADD eggs and work into a smooth dough.
DIVIDE dough in half.
ROLL each half to a 3 mm ($^1/_8$") thickness.
PLACE one-half of the dough on prepared baking sheet.

Filling:
DICE figs, dates and prunes. Place in large bowl.
ADD raisins and currants. Mix well. Pour rum over surface of fruit mixture.
COVER and let rest.
PREHEAT oven to 165°C (325°F).
STIR in walnuts and marmalade.
SPREAD filling evenly over dough on baking sheet.
COVER with second layer of dough.
PRICK dough with a fork and brush with milk.
BAKE for 20-25 minutes.
REMOVE from baking sheet.
COOL completely.
SLICE.

Turkish Treats

Recipe No. 634

Ingredients:

3	egg whites	3	
220 g	icing sugar, sifted	2 cups	
70 g	walnuts, ground	3/4 cup	

Dusting:

cocoa

Variation

Cream Filling:

125 mL	whipping cream	1/2 cup	
125 g	semi-sweet chocolate, chopped	5 squares	
1 pkg	**oetker** vanilla sugar	1 pkg	

PREHEAT oven to 120°C (250°F). Lightly grease a baking sheet.

BEAT egg whites to very stiff peaks. (Peaks should be so stiff that when a knife is inserted, the cut remains visible.)

ADD icing sugar, one tablespoon at a time.

BEAT until sugar has completely dissolved (approximately 15 minutes).

FOLD in walnuts, gently but thoroughly.

DROP from a teaspoon onto prepared baking sheet.

DUST lightly with cocoa.

BAKE for 40 minutes.

Variation
Cream Filling:

IN a saucepan, combine whipping cream, chocolate and vanilla sugar.

STIRRING constantly, heat mixture over medium heat until chocolate has melted.

POUR mixture into a mixing bowl. Chill.

USING an electric mixer, beat the chilled mixture for 2-3 minutes.

SPREAD filling on the underside of half of the cookies. Cover with remaining cookies.

Gingerbread Pretzels

Recipe No. 635

Dough:

175 mL	honey	³/₄ cup	
120 g	sugar	¹/₂ cup	
65 mL	water	¹/₃ cup	
	juice of ¹/₂ lemon		
1 pkg	**oetker** vanilla sugar	1 pkg	
5 drops	**oetker** lemon flavouring concentrate	5 drops	
300 g	whole wheat flour	2¹/₄ cups	
225 g	rye flour	2 cups	
1 pkg	**oetker** baking powder	1 pkg	
5 mL	baking soda	1 tsp	
5 mL	cinnamon	1 tsp	
1 mL	ginger	¹/₄ tsp	
1 mL	nutmeg	¹/₄ tsp	
2 mL	cloves, ground	¹/₂ tsp	
2	eggs	2	

Glaze:

1 pkg	**oetker** Chocofix	1 pkg	

LIGHTLY grease a baking sheet.
IN a saucepan, combine honey, sugar and water. Bring to a boil.
POUR into a mixing bowl.
ADD lemon juice, vanilla sugar and flavouring. Fold in gently but thoroughly.
CHILL mixture.
MIX together flours, baking powder, baking soda and spices.
SIFT over honey mixture. Work into a smooth dough.
LET rest for one hour.
PREHEAT oven to 180°C (350°F).
ADD eggs to mixture, mix well.
ROLL dough 3-6 mm (¹/₈-¹/₄") thick. Cut into strips.
SHAPE strips into pretzels. Place on prepared baking sheet.
BAKE for 12-15 minutes.
REMOVE pretzels from baking sheet. Cool completely.

Glaze:
PREPARE Chocofix according to package directions.
IMMERSE pretzels in glaze.

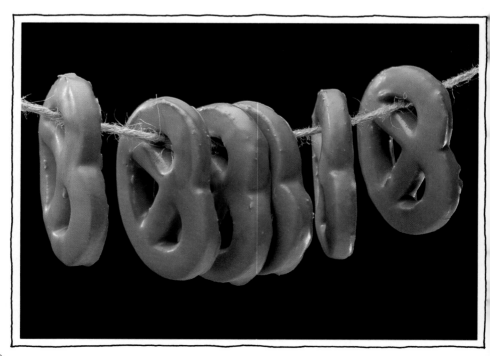

Jam Filled Crescents

Recipe No. 636

Ingredients:

380 g	marzipan	13½ oz	
200 g	icing sugar, sifted	1⅔ cups	
3	egg whites	3	
50 g	candied orange peel, finely chopped	¼ cup	
	grated peel of ½ lemon		

Filling:

45-60 mL	orange marmalade	3-4 tbsp	

Glaze:

1 pkg	**oetker** Chocofix	1 pkg	

LIGHTLY grease a baking sheet.
IN a mixing bowl, combine marzipan, icing sugar and egg whites.
BEAT until mixture is smooth and lump-free.
BLEND in candied orange peel and lemon peel.
PLACE mixture in a pastry bag fitted with a small round tube.
PIPE small crescents onto prepared baking sheet.
LET rest in the refrigerator for one to two hours.
PREHEAT oven to 175°C (350°F).
BAKE for 12 minutes.
REMOVE crescents from baking sheet. Cool completely.

Filling:
SPREAD marmalade on the underside of half of the crescents. Cover with remaining crescents.

Glaze:
PREPARE Chocofix according to package directions.
DIP the end of each crescent into the glaze.

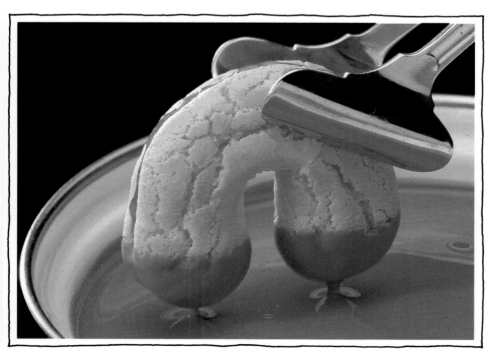

71

Rum Delicacies

Recipe No. 637

Dough:

300 g	all-purpose flour	2¼	cups
1 mL	**oetker** baking powder	¼	tsp
pinch	salt		pinch
100 g	icing sugar, sifted	¾	cup
1 pkg	**oetker** vanilla sugar	1	pkg
1	egg	1	
2 drops	**oetker** lemon flavouring concentrate	2	drops
220 g	butter or margarine, cold	1	cup

Macaroon Mixture:

3	egg whites	3	
200 g	sugar	1	cup
1 mL	cinnamon	¼	tsp
100 g	almonds, ground	1	cup

Cream Filling:

125 mL	whipping cream	½	cup
125 g	semi-sweet chocolate, chopped	5	squares

Jam Filling:

15 mL	plum jam	1	tbsp
15 mL	black currant jam	1	tbsp
½ btl	**oetker** rum flavouring concentrate	½	btl

Dipping:

1 pkg	**oetker** Chocofix	1	pkg

Topping:

almonds and pistachio nuts

MIX together flour and baking powder.
SIFT onto a working surface.
MAKE a well in the centre. Put salt, icing sugar, vanilla sugar, egg and flavouring in the well.
CUT butter or margarine in small pieces over the ingredients in the well.
COVER with flour.
STARTING from the centre, work all ingredients into a smooth dough.
CHILL for one-half hour.
PREHEAT oven to 180°C (350°F).
ROLL out dough thinly.
USING a round cookie cutter, cut out slices 5 cm (2") in diameter.
PLACE slices on baking sheet.

BAKE for 12-14 minutes.
AFTER 5 minutes of baking remove one-half of the slices from the baking sheet. Continue to bake the remaining half for an additional 7-8 minutes.
REMOVE cookies from baking sheet. Cool completely.

Macaroon Mixture:

REDUCE oven temperature to 160°C (325°F).
IN a mixing bowl, beat egg whites until frothy.
GRADUALLY beat in sugar and cinnamon.
CONTINUE beating until mass is stiff.
FOLD in almonds.
PLACE mixture in a pastry bag fitted with a small round tube.
PIPE rings on the cookies baked for 5 minutes.
PLACE cookies on baking sheet.
BAKE for 10-12 minutes.

Cream Filling:

IN a saucepan, combine whipping cream and chocolate.
STIRRING constantly, heat mixture over medium heat until chocolate has melted.
POUR mixture into a mixing bowl. Chill.
USING an electric mixer, beat chilled mixture for 2-3 minutes.
PLACE mixture in a pastry bag fitted with a small round tube.
PIPE onto the slices without the macaroon mixture.
TOP with slices with macaroon mixture.

Jam Filling:

COMBINE jams and flavouring. Mix well.
SPOON mixture into rings.

Dipping:

PREPARE Chocofix according to package directions.
GLAZE surface of cookies.
TOP with almonds and pistachio nuts.

Chocolate "S"

Recipe No. 638

Ingredients:

200 g	sugar	1 cup
50 mL	water	¼ cup
5	egg whites	5
50 g	icing sugar, sifted	½ cup
25 g	cocoa	¼ cup

PREHEAT oven to 120°C (250°F). Lightly grease a baking sheet.

IN a saucepan, combine sugar and water.

BRING to boil while stirring.

BEAT egg whites until frothy. Gradually beat in icing sugar.

CONTINUE beating until mass is stiff.

ADD sugar-water mixture to the egg whites, stirring constantly.

FOLD in cocoa gently but thoroughly.

PLACE mixture in a pastry bag fitted with a small round tube.

PIPE "S" shapes onto prepared baking sheet.

BAKE for 40-60 minutes.

Coconut Macaroons

Recipe No. 639

Ingredients:

5	egg whites	5
2 mL	cream of tartar	½ tsp
1 pkg	**oetker** vanilla sugar	1 pkg
5 drops	**oetker** lemon flavouring concentrate	5 drops
390 g	sugar	2 cups
280 g	dessicated coconut	3 cups
50 g	candied lemon - orange peel, finely chopped	⅓ cup

PREHEAT oven to 100°C (200°F). Lightly grease a baking sheet.

IN a mixing bowl, beat egg whites until foamy. Add cream of tartar, vanilla sugar and flavouring, continue beating.

GRADUALLY beat in sugar. Beat until sugar has dissolved.

FOLD in coconut and lemon - orange peel.

DROP by the teaspoon onto prepared baking sheet.

BAKE for one hour. Turn oven off. Leave macaroons in oven, overnight, to dry.

Fruit and Nut Slices

Recipe No. 640

Batter:

4	eggs	4		
30	mL	butter, melted	2	tbsp
280	g	icing sugar, sifted	2¼	cups
2	pkgs	**oetker** vanilla sugar	2	pkgs
1	btl	**oetker** lemon flavouring concentrate	1	btl
320	g	all-purpose flour	2¼	cups
½	pkg	**oetker** baking powder	½	pkg
80	g	nuts, chopped	⅔	cup
50	g	candied lemon peel, chopped	⅓	cup
50	g	candied orange peel, chopped	⅓	cup
60	g	raisins	⅓	cup
50	g	candied cherries	⅓	cup

PREHEAT oven to 175°C (350°F). Lightly grease a baking sheet.

IN a mixing bowl, combine eggs, butter, icing sugar, vanilla sugar and flavouring.

BEAT until thick and fluffy.

MIX together flour and baking powder.

SIFT over egg mixture. Mix well.

STIR in nuts, candied lemon and orange peel, raisins, and cherries.

SPREAD mixture 1 cm (³/₈") thick on prepared baking sheet.

BAKE 15-20 minutes.

CUT warm pastry into small bars.

Oatmeal Kisses

Recipe No. 641

Ingredients:

110	g	butter, softened	¹/₂ cup
100	g	icing sugar, sifted	³/₄ cup
1	pkg	**oetker** vanilla sugar	1 pkg
¹/₂	btl	**oetker** lemon flavouring concentrate	¹/₂ btl
1		egg	1
50	g	all-purpose flour	¹/₃ cup
150	g	rolled oats	1²/₃ cups
1	mL	cinnamon	¹/₄ tsp

PREHEAT oven to 180°C (350°F).
IN a mixing bowl, combine butter, icing sugar, vanilla sugar, flavouring and egg.
BEAT until fluffy.
SIFT flour over butter mixture. Mix well.
FOLD rolled oats and cinnamon into the mixture.
DROP from a teaspoon onto a baking sheet.
BAKE for 10 minutes.

Glazed Almond Rectangles

Recipe No. 642

Dough:

300 g	all-purpose flour	2	cups
1 mL	**oetker** baking powder	$^1/_4$	tsp
pinch	salt		pinch
120 g	icing sugar, sifted	1	cup
1 pkg	**oetker** vanilla sugar	1	pkg
3 drops	**oetker** lemon flavouring concentrate	3	drops
1	egg	1	
30 mL	milk	2	tbsp
220 g	butter or margarine, cold	1	cup

Filling:

120 g	sugar	$^1/_2$	cup
110 g	butter	$^1/_2$	cup
50 mL	honey	$^1/_4$	cup
250 g	almonds, slivered	2	cups
1 pkg	**oetker** vanilla sugar	1	pkg

Glaze:

150 g	milk chocolate, chopped	6	squares

Decoration:

	almonds, halved

LINE a baking sheet with parchment paper.
MIX together flour and baking powder.
SIFT onto a working surface.
MAKE a well in the centre. Put salt, icing sugar, vanilla sugar, flavouring, egg and milk in the well.
WORK into a thick paste.
CUT the butter or margarine in small pieces over the flour mixture.
STARTING from the centre, work all ingredients into a smooth dough.
CHILL for one-half hour.
PREHEAT oven to 180°C (350°F).
DIVIDE dough into two equal parts.
ROLL each half to a 3 mm ($^1/_8$") thickness.
PLACE one half on prepared baking sheet.

Filling:

IN a saucepan, combine sugar, butter and honey.
HEAT until mixture comes to a boil.
STIR in almonds and vanilla sugar.
LET cool slightly.
SPREAD honey mixture over surface of dough on baking sheet.
COVER with remaining dough layer. Gently press down.
BAKE for 18 minutes.
REMOVE from baking sheet. Cool completely.
SLICE into rectangles.

Glaze:

MELT chocolate in a double boiler.
GLAZE rectangles.
DECORATE with almonds.

(**TIP**: Place pastry on a fork and dip into the chocolate. Place on waxed paper. Cool completely.)

Cinnamon Almond Cookies

Recipe No. 643

Dough:

220 g	butter or margarine, softened	1	cup
120 g	icing sugar, sifted	1	cup
1 pkg	**oetker** vanilla sugar	1	pkg
¹/₂ btl	**oetker** lemon flavouring concentrate	¹/₂	btl
pinch	salt		pinch
1	egg	1	
225 g	all-purpose flour	1³/₄	cups
70 g	**oetker** Gustin corn starch	¹/₂	cup
5 mL	**oetker** baking powder	1	tsp

Brushing:

1	egg white, beaten	1	

Sprinkling:

5-10 mL	cinnamon	1-2	tsp
15 mL	coarse sugar	1	tbsp
50 g	almonds, chopped	¹/₃	cup

LIGHTLY grease a baking sheet.
IN a mixing bowl, whip butter until fluffy.
GRADUALLY add icing sugar, vanilla sugar, flavouring, salt and egg.
MIX together flour, corn starch and baking powder.
SIFT over butter mixture. Knead quickly into a smooth dough.
CHILL for one-half hour.
PREHEAT oven to 180°C (350°F).
ROLL out dough to a 3 mm (¹/₈") thickness.
USING a round cookie cutter, cut out slices 5 cm (2") in diameter.
PLACE slices on prepared baking sheet.
BRUSH with egg white.

Sprinkling:
MIX together cinnamon, sugar and almonds.
SPRINKLE on slices.
BAKE for 10 minutes.

Almond Bites

Recipe No. 644

Dough:

300 g	all-purpose flour	1³/₄	cups
1 mL	**oetker** baking powder	¹/₄	tsp
120 g	icing sugar, sifted	1	cup
1	egg	1	
1	egg yolk	1	
¹/₂ btl	**oetker** lemon flavouring concentrate	¹/₂	btl
165 g	butter or margarine, cold	³/₄	cup

Topping:

150 g	almonds, sliced	1¹/₂	cups
1	egg white	1	
15 mL	kirsch (cherry brandy)	1	tbsp

LIGHTLY grease a baking sheet.
MIX together flour and baking powder.
SIFT onto a working surface.
MAKE a well in the centre. Put icing sugar, egg, egg yolk and flavouring in the well.
CUT butter or margarine in small pieces over the ingredients in the well.
COVER with flour.
STARTING from the centre, work all ingredients into a smooth dough.
CHILL for one hour.
PREHEAT oven to 200°C (400°F).
ROLL out dough thinly.
PLACE dough on prepared baking sheet.

Topping:
IN a mixing bowl, combine almonds, egg white and kirsch. Mix well.
SPREAD mixture evenly over dough.
CHILL for one hour.
CUT into slices.
BAKE for 8-10 minutes.

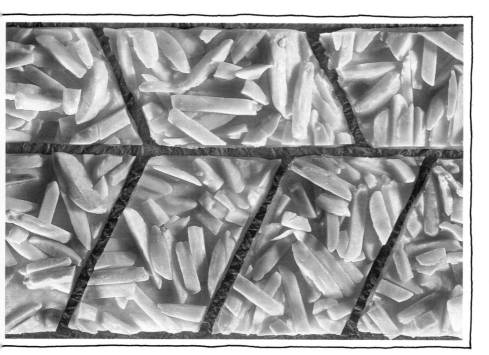

Elisen Gingerbread

Recipe No. 645

Dough:

375 g	sugar	1³/₄	cups
250 g	nuts, ground	2²/₃	cups
4	egg whites	4	
200 g	all-purpose flour	1¹/₂	cups
125 g	candied orange peel, diced	1	cup
80 g	candied lemon peel, diced	¹/₂	cup
15 mL	cinnamon	1	tbsp
2 mL	cloves, ground	¹/₂	tsp
2 mL	allspice	¹/₂	tsp
5 mL	nutmeg	1	tsp
5 mL	baking soda	1	tsp
some	round baking wafers (6 cm diameter)	some	

Glaze:

some	**oetker** Chocofix	some

Decoration:

icing sugar, sifted
almonds, halved,
coloured sprinkles

LINE a baking sheet with parchment paper.
IN a mixing bowl, combine sugar, nuts and egg whites.
PLACE bowl in a water bath.
STIRRING constantly, heat until mixture reaches a temperature of 50°C (125°F).
REMOVE bowl from water bath. Continue stirring until nut mixture is lukewarm.
ADD flour, candied orange and lemon peel, spices, and baking soda.
KNEAD well.
SPREAD the dough in a dome-shaped fashion on the baking wafers.
SMOOTH out with a wet knife. Top half of the gingerbread with sliced almonds.
PLACE gingerbread on prepared baking sheet.
LET rest overnight in the refrigerator.
PREHEAT oven to 200°C (400°F).
BAKE for 25 minutes.
COOL completely.

Glaze:
PREPARE Chocofix according to package directions.
GLAZE cooled gingerbread.
DECORATE with icing sugar, almonds and coloured sprinkles.

Marzipan Filled Crescents

Recipe No. 646

Dough:

250 mL	honey	1	cup
150 g	sugar	³/₄	cup
45 mL	water	3	tbsp
500 g	all-purpose flour	3¹/₂	cups
5 mL	baking soda	1	tsp
2 mL	nutmeg	¹/₂	tsp
2 mL	allspice	¹/₂	tsp
5 mL	cinnamon	1	tsp
1 mL	cloves, ground	¹/₄	tsp
30 mL	kirsch (cherry brandy)	2	tbsp
¹/₂ btl	**oetker** lemon flavouring concentrate	¹/₂	btl

Filling:

150 g	marzipan	5¹/₂	oz
30 mL	icing sugar, sifted	2	tbsp
some	kirsch (cherry brandy)		some

Brushing:

1	egg	1	
15 mL	milk	1	tbsp

LINE a baking sheet with parchment paper.
IN a saucepan, combine honey, sugar and water. Bring to a quick boil.
POUR mixture into a mixing bowl. Chill.
MIX together flour and baking soda.
SIFT over honey mixture.
SPRINKLE spices over the mixture.
ADD kirsch and flavouring.
KNEAD mixture well.
CHILL for one hour.
PREHEAT oven to 200°C (400°F).
ROLL out dough to a 1 cm (³/₈") thickness. Divide in two.

Filling:
COMBINE marzipan, icing sugar and kirsch, to taste. Knead well.
SHAPE into two rolls.
PLACE the marzipan rolls on top of the two halves. Roll up each half tightly.
USING a knife, cut the rolls into slices.
STAND slices on prepared baking sheet.
WHISK together egg and milk.
BRUSH each slice with egg mixture.
BAKE for 12 minutes.

*B*utter Balls

Recipe No. 647

Dough:

200 g	butter, softened	³/₄	cup
120 g	icing sugar, sifted	1	cup
2 pkgs	**oetker** vanilla sugar	2	pkgs
¹/₂ btl	**oetker** lemon flavouring concentrate	¹/₂	btl
pinch	salt		pinch
1	egg	1	
250 g	all-purpose flour	1³/₄	cups
30 g	**oetker** Gustin corn starch	¹/₄	cup

Decoration:

some	**oetker** Chocofix	some	

PREHEAT oven to 190°C (375°F).
IN a mixing bowl, combine butter, icing sugar, vanilla sugar, flavouring, salt and egg.
BEAT until fluffy.
MIX together flour and corn starch.
SIFT over butter mixture. Fold in gently but thoroughly.
PUT mixture in a pastry bag fitted with a round tube.
PIPE walnut size portions onto baking sheet.
FLATTEN.
BAKE for 8-10 minutes. Cool completely.
PREPARE Chocofix according to package directions
PLACE in a small pastry bag, fitted with a small tube.
DRIZZLE chocolate on surface of cookies.

Meringue Rings

Recipe No. 648

Ingredients:

3	egg whites	3	
1 mL	cream of tartar	¹/₄ tsp	
110 g	sugar	¹/₂ cup	
1 pkg	**oetker** vanilla sugar	1 pkg	
some	food colouring	some	

Sprinkling:

sprinkles or coloured sugar

PREHEAT oven to 120°C (250°F). Line a baking sheet with parchment paper.
BEAT egg whites until frothy.
SIFT cream of tartar over surface, continue beating.
GRADUALLY beat in sugar and vanilla sugar.
CONTINUE beating until the sugar has dissolved and mixture is stiff.
ADD food colouring, as desired.
PLACE mixture in a pastry bag fitted with a star tube.
PIPE rings onto prepared baking sheet.
SPRINKLE with coloured sugar or sprinkles.
BAKE for 40-60 minutes.

Spicy Squares

Recipe No. 649

Dough:

250 mL	honey	1 cup
150 g	sugar	$^2/_3$ cup
450 g	all-purpose flour	$3^1/_4$ cups
1 pkg	**oetker** baking powder	1 pkg
5 mL	baking soda	1 tsp
50 g	candied lemon peel	$^1/_3$ cup
50 g	candied orange peel	$^1/_3$ cup
15 mL	cinnamon	1 tbsp
2 mL	cloves, ground	$^1/_2$ tsp
2 mL	allspice	$^1/_2$ tsp
2 mL	nutmeg	$^1/_2$ tsp
1 btl	**oetker** lemon flavouring concentrate	1 btl
1 shot	kirsch (cherry brandy)	1 shot
45 mL	milk	3 tbsp
2	eggs	2

Glaze:

| 120 g | icing sugar | 1 cup |
| 15-30 mL | hot water | 1-2 tbsp |

PREHEAT oven to 190°C (375°F). Grease and flour a baking sheet.
IN a saucepan, combine honey and sugar. HEAT.
POUR into a large mixing bowl.
ADD flour, baking powder, baking soda, candied lemon and orange peel, spices, flavouring, kirsch and milk.
MIX well. Add eggs. Knead dough.
ROLL out dough to a 6-7 cm (2$^1/_4$-2$^3/_4$") thickness.
PLACE on prepared baking sheet.
BAKE for 20-25 minutes.

Glaze:
SIFT icing sugar into a mixing bowl.
ADD water and stir into a thick paste.
BRUSH warm pastry with glaze.
COOL completely.
SLICE into pieces.

Savoury Biscuits

Fancy Crackers

Recipe No. 650

Ingredients:
1-150 g pkg poppy seed and/   1-150 g pkg
or sesame crackers

Cheese Filling:

60	g	butter, softened	¼ cup
125	g	pepper-cream cheese	125 g
15	mL	whipping cream	1 tbsp

Topping:

cubed ham, chopped
parsley, yellow pepper,
radishes, sliced olives, etc.

BEAT butter until fluffy.
ADD cream cheese and whipping cream. Beat
until mixture is smooth.
SPREAD mixture on half of the crackers. Top
with remaining crackers.
DECORATE as desired.

Gorgonzola Crackers

Recipe No. 652

Ingredients:
2-150 g pkgs vegetable   2-150 g pkgs
crackers

Cheese Filling:

110	g	butter, softened	½ cup
120	g	gorgonzola, room temperature	¾ cup
1	clove	garlic, minced	1 clove
15	mL	whipping cream	1 tbsp

Topping:

chives, red pepper,
stuffed olives, etc.

BEAT butter until fluffy.
ADD cheese, garlic and whipping cream. Beat
until mixture is smooth.
SPREAD mixture on half of the crackers. Top
with remaining crackers.
DECORATE as desired.

Cream Cheese Crackers

Recipe No. 651

Ingredients:
1-150 g pkg cheese crackers   1-150 g pkg

Cheese Filling:

55	g	butter, softened	¼ cup
125	g	cream cheese with herbs	125 g
1		small onion, finely chopped	1
5	mL	chives, finely chopped	1 tsp
15	mL	sour cream	1 tbsp
50	g	quark cheese	¼ cup

Topping:

chopped egg, red and
green pepper, etc.

BEAT butter until fluffy.
ADD cream cheese, onion, chives, sour cream
and quark.
BEAT until mixture is smooth.
SPREAD mixture on half of the crackers. Top
with remaining crackers.
DECORATE as desired.

Filled Gorgonzola Bars

Recipe No. 653

Pastry:

1	pkg	frozen puff pastry	1 pkg

Brushing:

1		egg, whisked	1

Cheese Filling:

100	g	gorgonzola	²/₃ cup
55	g	butter, softened	¹/₄ cup
15	mL	whipping cream	1 tbsp

Topping:

cheese filling (above), parsley, olives, grapes, paprika

PREHEAT oven to 200°C (400°F).
THAW puff pastry according to package directions.
ROLL out thinly.
CUT into 8 x 3 cm (3 x 1") bars.
BRUSH with egg.
PLACE bars on baking sheet.
BAKE for 10-15 minutes.

Cheese Filling:

PUT gorgonzola into a mixing bowl. Add butter and whipping cream. Beat until fluffy. (Set aside some cheese mixture for decorating.)
PLACE cheese mixture in a pastry bag fitted with a star tube.
PIPE filling on the underside of half of the bars. Top with remaining bars.
DECORATE with reserved cheese mixture, parsley, olives, etc.

Cheesy Spirals

Recipe No. 654

Pastry:

1	pkg	frozen puff pastry	1 pkg

Brushing:

1		egg, lightly beaten	1

Cheese Filling:

100 g		emmenthal cheese, grated	1 cup
30 g		parmesan cheese, grated	1/4 cup
		paprika, cayenne pepper, salt	

Sprinkling:

parmesan cheese, grated

PREHEAT oven to 200°C (400°F).
THAW puff pastry according to package directions.
ROLL out thinly. Divide in two.
LIGHTLY brush with egg.

Cheese Filling:

MIX together emmenthal and parmesan cheese.
ADD paprika, cayenne pepper and salt, to taste.
SPREAD cheese mixture evenly over one-half of the pastry.
TOP with remaining half.
USING a rolling pin, lightly press pastry together.
BRUSH surface of pastry with remaining egg.
SPRINKLE with parmesan cheese. Slice into 2 cm (1") wide strips.
SHAPE each strip into a spiral. Place on baking sheet.
BAKE for 15 minutes.

Cheese Puffs

Recipe No. 655

Dough:

250	mL	water	1 cup
110	g	butter	$^1/_2$ cup
1	mL	salt	$^1/_4$ tsp
135	g	all-purpose flour	1 cup
4		eggs	4

Cheese Filling:

125	mL	milk	$^1/_2$ cup
15	mL	**oetker** Gustin corn starch	1 tbsp
15	mL	parmesan cheese, grated	1 tbsp
2	mL	salt	$^1/_2$ tsp
		pinch nutmeg, white pepper	pinch
110	g	butter, softened	$^1/_2$ cup
30	mL	emmenthal cheese, finely grated	2 tbsp

Topping:

cream cheese filling, reserved dough ornaments

IN a saucepan, bring water, butter and salt to a boil.

REMOVE from heat and add flour all at once.
STIR over medium heat until mixture forms a ball around the spoon and pulls away from the sides of the pan. (Do not overcook.) Cool slightly.

ADD unbeaten eggs to dough one at a time, stirring after each addition until smooth.
Continue stirring until mixture is shiny and no longer sticky. Chill until mixture holds its shape.

PREHEAT oven to 220°C (425°F).

SET a small portion of the mixture aside to prepare dough ornaments.

PLACE remaining mixture in a pastry bag fitted with a star tube.

SQUEEZE portions, the size of a walnut, onto an ungreased baking sheet.

BAKE for 25 - 30 minutes. (Do not open oven door during first 15 minutes of baking, pastry may collapse.)

Dough Ornaments:

PUT the reserved mixture into a pastry bag.
SQUEEZE dough ornaments onto baking sheet.
BAKE for 6 minutes.

Cheese Filling:

PLACE milk in a saucepan. Add corn starch.
STIR over medium heat until mixture comes to a boil.
ADD parmesan cheese, salt, nutmeg and pepper. Mix well.
COOL completely.
BEAT butter until fluffy.
ADD cheese mixture, one spoonful at a time.
STIR in emmenthal cheese.
PLACE cheese mixture in a pastry bag fitted with a round tube.
WITH a sharp knife make a small incision in the lower half of each pastry.
FILL with cheese mixture.

Filled Cheese Savouries

Dough:

400 g	all-purpose flour	3	cups
1 pkg	**oetker** baking powder	1	pkg
200 g	emmenthal cheese, grated	2	cups
2 mL	salt	$^1/_2$	tsp
2	eggs	2	
330 g	butter or margarine, cold	$1^1/_2$	cups

Basic Cream Cheese Filling:

375 mL	milk	$1^1/_2$	cups
40 g	**oetker** Gustin corn starch	$^1/_4$	cup
70 g	parmesan, grated	$^1/_2$	cup
	salt, nutmeg, white pepper		
2	egg yolks	2	
330 g	butter, softened	$1^1/_2$	cups

Cream Cheese Filling — Variation:

1 clove	garlic, minced	1	clove
1	egg yolk, finely chopped	1	
1	anchovy, grated	1	
2	small onions, finely chopped	2	
60 g	cream cheese	60	g
15 mL	herbs, finely chopped	1	tbsp

Toppings:

stuffed olives, chopped egg white, parsley, radishes, red pepper, chives, hard-boiled egg yolk, finely chopped, grapes, nuts, etc.

MIX together flour and baking powder.
SIFT onto a working surface.
MAKE a well in the centre. Put cheese, salt and eggs in the well.
WORK into a thick paste.
CUT the butter or margarine in small pieces over the mixture.
STARTING from the centre, work all ingredients into a smooth dough.
WRAP dough in aluminum foil and chill for two hours.
PREHEAT oven to 190°C (375°F).
ROLL out dough to a 2-3 mm ($^1/_{16}$ - $^1/_8$") thickness.
USING cookie cutters, cut out desired shapes.
PLACE biscuits on prepared baking sheet.
BAKE on middle oven rack for 10 minutes.

Basic Cream Cheese Filling:

POUR milk into a saucepan.
ADD corn starch. Stir over medium heat until mixture comes to a boil.
COOL slightly.
FOLD in parmesan cheese, salt, nutmeg and pepper, to taste, and egg yolks, gently but thoroughly.
CHILL mixture.
BEAT butter until fluffy.
ADD the chilled mixture, one spoonful at a time.

Cream Cheese Filling — Variation:

DIVIDE the basic cream cheese filling into six small bowls. Add ingredients listed.
SPREAD filling on the underside of half of the biscuits.
TOP with remaining biscuits.
DECORATE as desired.

97

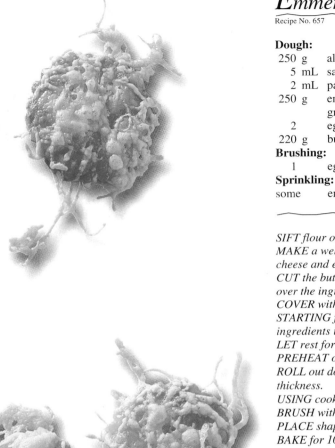

Emmenthal Biscuits

Recipe No. 657

Dough:

250 g	all-purpose flour	1³/₄ cups
5 mL	salt	1 tsp
2 mL	paprika	¹/₂ tsp
250 g	emmenthal cheese, grated	2¹/₂ cups
2	eggs	2
220 g	butter or margarine, cold	1 cup

Brushing:

1	egg, lightly beaten	1

Sprinkling:

some	emmenthal cheese, grated	some

SIFT flour onto a working surface.
MAKE a well in the centre. Put salt, paprika, cheese and eggs in the well.
CUT the butter or margarine in small pieces over the ingredients in the well.
COVER with flour.
STARTING from the centre, work all ingredients into a smooth dough.
LET rest for one hour.
PREHEAT oven to 190°C (375°F).
ROLL out dough evenly to a 3 mm (¹/₈") thickness.
USING cookie cutters, cut out desired shapes.
BRUSH with egg. Sprinkle with cheese.
PLACE shapes on baking sheet.
BAKE for 10 minutes.

Caraway Seed Sticks

Recipe No. 658

Dough:

500	g	all-purpose flour	3½	cups
1	pkg	**oetker** instant dry yeast	1	pkg
2	mL	salt	½	tsp
1	mL	caraway seeds, ground	¼	tsp
185	mL	cold milk	¾	cup
275	g	butter, softened	1¼	cups

Brushing:

1		egg, lightly beaten	1

Sprinkling:

caraway seeds
salt

SIFT flour into a mixing bowl. Add yeast and mix well.

MAKE a well in the centre. Put salt, caraway seeds and milk in the well.

ADD butter. Knead with an electric mixer fitted with dough hooks until smooth, blistery and no longer sticky.

COVER dough and chill for one-half hour.

ROLL out dough thinly (3 mm / ⅛"). Place on baking sheet.

CUT into 1 x 6 cm (⅜ x 2¼") long pieces.

COVER and let rest at room temperature for 15 minutes.

PREHEAT oven to 190°C (375°F).

BRUSH with egg. Sprinkle with caraway seeds and salt.

BAKE for 12 minutes.

Savouries

Recipe No. 659

Dough:

250 g	all-purpose flour	1³/₄	cups
15 mL	**oetker** baking powder	1	tbsp
5 mL	salt	1	tsp
1	egg yolk	1	
45 mL	water	3	tbsp
110 g	butter or margarine, cold	¹/₂	cup

Brushing:

1	egg white, lightly beaten	1

Sprinkling:

caraway seeds, poppy seeds, grated cheese, coarse salt

MIX together flour and baking powder.
SIFT onto a working surface.
MAKE a well in the centre. Put salt, egg yolk and water in the well.
WORK into a thick paste.
CUT butter or margarine in small pieces over the mixture.
STARTING from the centre, work all ingredients into a smooth dough.
CHILL for one-half hour.
PREHEAT oven to 180°C (350°F).
ROLL out two-thirds of the dough thinly (3 mm / ¹/₈").
USING cookie cutters, cut out desired shapes.
BRUSH with egg white.
SPRINKLE with caraway seeds, poppy seeds or cheese.
PLACE on baking sheet.
ROLL out remaining dough thinly (3 mm / ¹/₈").
CUT into 1 x 8 cm (³/₈ x 3") strips.
SHAPE strips into spirals.
BRUSH with egg white.
SPRINKLE with salt.
PLACE on baking sheet.
BAKE for 12-15 minutes.

Caraway Pretzels

Recipe No. 660

Dough:

200 g	all-purpose flour	1 1/2	cups
5 mL	**oetker** baking powder	1	tsp
2 mL	salt	1/2	tsp
45 mL	sour cream	3	tbsp
165 g	butter or margarine, cold	3/4	cup

Brushing:

1	egg yolk	1	
15 mL	milk	1	tbsp

Sprinkling:

50 mL	caraway seeds	1/4	cup

MIX together flour and baking powder.
SIFT onto a working surface.
MAKE a well in the centre. Put salt and sour cream in the well.
CUT butter or margarine in small pieces over the ingredients in the well.
COVER with flour.
STARTING from the centre, work all ingredients into a smooth dough.
CHILL for one-half hour.
PREHEAT oven to 180°C (350°F).
SHAPE dough into rolls the thickness of a pencil.
CUT into 13 cm (5") long pieces.
SHAPE pieces into pretzels.
PLACE pretzels on baking sheet.
BEAT egg yolk with milk.
BRUSH pretzels with egg yolk mixture.
SPRINKLE with caraway seeds.
BAKE for 10-15 minutes.

Family Favourites

Three-Cornered Hats

Recipe No. 661

Dough:

350 g	all-purpose flour	2²/₃ cups
5 mL	**oetker** baking powder	1 tsp
125 mL	sour cream	¹/₂ cup
2	egg yolks	2
1 mL	salt	¹/₄ tsp
60 g	sugar	¹/₄ cup
220 g	butter or margarine, cold	1 cup

Filling:

100 g	hazelnuts, ground	1 cup
4 drops	**oetker** rum flavouring concentrate	4 drops
60 g	sugar	¹/₄ cup
30 mL	milk	2 tbsp
1	egg	1

Brushing:

some	milk	some

MIX together flour and baking powder.
SIFT onto a working surface.
COMBINE sour cream and egg yolks. Mix well.
MAKE a well in the centre. Put sour cream - egg yolk mixture, salt and sugar in the well.
CUT butter or margarine in small pieces over the ingredients in the well.
COVER with flour.
STARTING from the centre, work all ingredients into a smooth dough.
CHILL for one-half hour.
PREHEAT oven to 200°C (400°F).
ON a lightly floured surface roll out dough 3 mm (¹/₈") thick.
USING a round cookie cutter, cut out slices 5 cm (2") in diameter.

Filling:

IN a mixing bowl, combine hazelnuts, flavouring, sugar, milk and egg. Mix well.
PLACE a small amount of nut mixture in the centre of each slice.
PULL up the dough on three parts of the circle. Pinch to seal.
BRUSH with milk.
ARRANGE on baking sheet.
BAKE for 10 - 12 minutes.

Marble Rings

Recipe No. 662

Dough:

150	g	butter or margarine, softened	$^2/_3$ cup
140	g	sugar	$^2/_3$ cup
1	pkg	**oetker** vanilla sugar	1 pkg
2		eggs	2
250	g	all-purpose flour	$1^3/_4$ cups
2	mL	**oetker** baking powder	$^1/_2$ tsp
50	mL	cocoa	4 tbsp

PREHEAT oven to 190°C (375°F).
IN a mixing bowl, combine butter or margarine, sugar and vanilla sugar.
BEAT until fluffy. Add eggs, one at a time, beating well after each addition.
MIX together flour and baking powder.
SIFT over butter mixture. Fold in gently but thoroughly.
DIVIDE dough in thirds. To one-third of the dough, add cocoa. Mix well.
FOLD gently into remaining two-thirds dough.
PLACE dough in a pastry bag fitted with a large star tube.
SQUEEZE rings onto baking sheet.
BAKE for 10-12 minutes.

*A*niseed Biscuits

Recipe No. 663

Dough:

75	g	butter or margarine, softened	¹/₃ cup
50	g	brown sugar	¹/₃ cup
5	mL	**oetker** vanilla sugar	1 tsp
2		egg yolks	2
135	g	all-purpose flour	1 cup
2	mL	**oetker** baking powder	¹/₂ tsp
1	mL	salt	¹/₄ tsp
10	mL	aniseed	2 tsp

Sprinkling:

aniseed

PREHEAT oven to 190°C (375°F). Lightly grease a baking sheet.

IN a mixing bowl, combine butter or margarine, brown sugar and vanilla sugar.

BEAT until fluffy.

ADD egg yolks, mix well.

MIX together flour, baking powder, salt and aniseed.

SIFT over butter mixture. Fold in gently but thoroughly.

DROP by the teaspoon onto prepared baking sheet.

SPRINKLE with aniseed.

BAKE for 10 minutes or until golden brown.

*A*lmond Raisin Rings

Recipe No. 664

Dough:

370	g	all-purpose flour	2³/₄ cups
30	mL	**oetker** Gustin corn starch	2 tbsp
2	mL	cream of tartar	¹/₂ tsp
2	mL	baking soda	¹/₂ tsp
200	g	sugar	1 cup
1		egg	1
40	g	almonds, ground	¹/₃ cup
125	mL	milk	¹/₂ cup
40	g	raisins, finely chopped	¹/₄ cup
110	g	butter or margarine, softened	¹/₂ cup

Brushing:

some	milk	some

LIGHTLY grease a baking sheet.
MIX together flour, corn starch, cream of tartar and baking soda.
SIFT onto a working surface.
MAKE a well in the centre. Put sugar, egg, almonds, milk and raisins in the well.
CUT butter or margarine in small pieces over the ingredients in the well.
COVER with flour.
STARTING from the centre, work all ingredients into a smooth dough.
CHILL for one-quarter hour.
PREHEAT oven to 190°C (375°F).
ON a lightly floured surface, roll out dough to a 4-6 mm (¹/₈ - ³/₁₆") thickness.
USING a round cookie cutter with scalloped edges, cut out slices 5 cm (2") in diameter.
PLACE rings on prepared baking sheet.
BRUSH with milk.
BAKE for 8-10 minutes.

*R*ed Currant Treats

Recipe No. 665

Dough:

150 g	all-purpose flour	1¼	cups
2 mL	**oetker** baking powder	½	tsp
50 g	sugar	¼	cup
1 pkg	**oetker** vanilla sugar	1	pkg
70 g	almonds, ground	¾	cup
1	egg yolk	1	
110 g	butter or margarine, cold	½	cup
60 g	cream cheese	⅓	cup

Filling:

50 mL	red currant jam	¼	cup

LIGHTLY grease a baking sheet.
MIX together flour and baking powder.
SIFT onto a working surface.
MAKE a well in the centre. Put sugar, vanilla sugar, almonds and egg yolk in the well.
CUT butter or margarine and cream cheese in small pieces over the ingredients in the well.
COVER with flour.
STARTING from the centre, work all ingredients into a smooth dough.
CHILL for one-half hour.
PREHEAT oven to 180°C (350°F).
SHAPE dough into balls the size of a walnut.
PLACE on prepared baking sheet.
MAKE a small well in the centre of each ball.
FILL with jam.
BAKE for 10-12 minutes.

*V*anilla Nut Slices

Recipe No. 666

Dough:

220 g	butter or margarine, softened	1	cup
100 g	sugar	½	cup
50 g	icing sugar, sifted	½	cup
1 pkg	**oetker** vanilla sugar	1	pkg
1	egg	1	
370 g	all-purpose flour	2¾	cups
2 mL	baking soda	½	tsp
2 mL	cream of tartar	½	tsp
50 g	**oetker** Gustin corn starch	⅓	cup
2 mL	cinnamon	½	tsp
30 g	almonds, ground	¼	cup

Filling:

125 mL	red currant jam	½	cup

IN a mixing bowl, combine butter or margarine, sugar, icing sugar and vanilla sugar. Beat until fluffy.
ADD egg, mix well.
MIX together flour, baking soda, cream of tartar and corn starch.
SIFT over butter mixture.
ADD cinnamon and almonds.
STARTING from the centre, work all ingredients into a smooth dough.
CHILL for one hour.
PREHEAT oven to 180°C (350°F).
ON a lightly floured surface, roll dough to a 3 mm (⅛") thickness.
USING a round cookie cutter, cut out slices 5 cm (2") in diameter.
CUT out small triangle shapes in the centre of half the cookies.
PLACE all slices on baking sheet
BAKE 10-12 minutes.
REMOVE cookies from baking sheet.
COOL completely.

Filling:

SPREAD jam on the underside of the slices without triangles.
TOP with slices with triangles. Press lightly to seal.

Choconut Mounds

Recipe No. 667

Dough:

220 g	butter or margarine, softened	1	cup
125 g	cream cheese, softened	125	g
300 g	sugar	1¹/₂	cups
4 drops	**oetker** orange flavouring concentrate	4	drops
2	eggs	2	
335 g	all-purpose flour	2¹/₂	cups
5 mL	**oetker** baking powder	1	tsp
35 g	cocoa	¹/₂	cup
50 g	hazelnuts, ground	¹/₂	cup

Decoration:

1 pkg	**oetker** Chocofix	1	pkg

PREHEAT oven to 190°C (375°F).

IN a mixing bowl, combine butter or margarine, cream cheese, sugar and flavouring.

BEAT until fluffy.

ADD eggs, beat until smooth.

MIX together flour, baking powder, cocoa and hazelnuts.

SIFT over butter mixture. Fold in quickly but thoroughly.

DROP mixture from a teaspoon, well apart, onto baking sheet.

BAKE for 10-12 minutes.

COOL before removing to wire rack. Cool completely.

PREPARE Chocofix according to package directions.

DRIZZLE chocolate over cookies.

Almond Stars

Recipe No. 668

Dough:

110 g	butter or margarine, cold	¹/₂	cup
80 g	sugar	¹/₃	cup
1 pkg	**oetker** vanilla sugar	1	pkg
2	egg yolks	2	
250 g	all-purpose flour	1³/₄	cups
10 mL	**oetker** baking powder	2	tsp
1 mL	salt	¹/₄	tsp
50 g	almonds, finely chopped	¹/₃	cup
15 mL	kirsch (cherry brandy)	1	tbsp

Brushing:

1	egg yolk	1	
30 mL	milk	2	tbsp

Dusting:

	icing sugar, sifted

IN a mixing bowl, combine butter or margarine, sugar and vanilla sugar. Beat until fluffy.

BEAT in egg yolks.

IN another bowl, sieve together flour, baking powder and salt. Add almonds and mix well.

STIR flour mixture into butter mixture alternately with kirsch.

MIX thoroughly. Work into a smooth dough.

CHILL for one-half hour.

PREHEAT oven to 180°C (350°F).

ON a lightly floured surface, roll out dough to a 4 mm (¹/₈") thickness.

USING a star-shaped cookie cutter, cut out shapes.

PLACE stars on baking sheet.

BEAT egg yolk with milk. Brush stars.

BAKE for 10-12 minutes.

COOL completely.

DUST with icing sugar.

*T*ea Crackers

Recipe No. 669

Dough:

250 g	all-purpose flour	1¾	cups
1 pkg	**oetker** instant dry yeast	1	pkg
1 mL	salt	¼	tsp
3 drops	**oetker** lemon flavouring concentrate	3	drops
3 drops	**oetker** rum flavouring concentrate	3	drops
1	egg	1	
165 g	butter or margarine, softened	¾	cup
30 mL	whipping cream	2	tbsp

Brushing:

1	egg, whisked	1	

PREHEAT oven to 200°C (400°F).
SIFT flour into a mixing bowl.
ADD yeast, mix well.
MAKE a well in the centre. Put salt, flavourings and egg in the well.
COVER with flour.
MIX the butter or margarine with the whipping cream.
ADD butter mixture to the flour.
WORK all ingredients into a smooth dough.
ROLL dough 4 mm (⅛") thick.
USING a variety of cookie cutters, cut out shapes.
PLACE shapes on baking sheet.
BRUSH with egg. Cover.
LET rest in a warm place for 10 minutes.
BAKE for 12 minutes.
COOL completely.

*O*atmeal Cookies

Recipe No. 670

Dough:

110 g	butter or margarine, softened	¹/₂	cup
100 g	sugar	¹/₂	cup
40 g	brown sugar	¹/₄	cup
1 pkg	**oetker** vanilla sugar	1	pkg
1	egg	1	
30 mL	milk	2	tbsp
150 g	all-purpose flour	1	cup
2 mL	**oetker** baking powder	¹/₂	tsp
2 mL	baking soda	¹/₂	tsp
pinch	salt		pinch
100 g	rolled oats	1	cup
50 g	almonds, ground	¹/₂	cup

Drizzling:

1 pkg	**oetker** Chocofix	1	pkg

IN a mixing bowl, combine butter or margarine, sugar, brown sugar and vanilla sugar. Beat until fluffy.

ADD egg and milk. Beat well.

MIX together flour, baking powder, baking soda and salt.

SIFT over butter mixture. Beat until well blended.

STIR in rolled oats and al:nonds.

CHILL for one hour.

PREHEAT oven to 190°C (375°F).

DROP by the teaspoon onto baking sheet.

SHAPE into 2.5 cm (1") balls.

BAKE for 10-12 minutes.

REMOVE cookies from baking sheet. Cool completely.

PREPARE Chocofix according to package directions.

DRIZZLE over cookies.

113

Cinnamon Stars

Recipe No. 671

Dough:

350 g	all-purpose flour	2¼	cups
pinch	**oetker** baking powder		pinch
100 g	sugar	½	cup
5 mL	cinnamon	1	tsp
2 mL	ginger, ground	½	tsp
200 g	butter or margarine	¾	cup
2	egg yolks	2	
1	egg	1	

Brushing:

1	egg yolk	1	
30 mL	milk	2	tbsp

Glaze:

150 g	icing sugar, sifted	1	cup
15-30 mL	water	1-2	tbsp

PREHEAT oven to 180°C (350°F).
IN a large bowl, with an electric mixer, mix first six ingredients until crumbly.
ADD egg yolks and whole egg to make a firm dough.
ON a lightly floured surface, roll dough to a 1 cm (⅜") thickness.
CUT dough with a star shaped cookie cutter.
PLACE stars on baking sheet.

Brushing:

MIX egg yolk with milk. Brush tops of cookies with egg mixture.
BAKE for 8 minutes.
COOL completely.

Glaze:

IN a small bowl, mix icing sugar and water until smooth.
GLAZE cookies.

Spicy Waffles

Recipe No. 672

Ingredients:

3	eggs	3
50 g	sugar	¼ cup
1 pkg	**oetker** vanilla sugar	1 pkg
225 g	all-purpose flour	1¾ cups
10 mL	**oetker** baking powder	2 tsp
1 mL	salt	¼ tsp
5 mL	cinnamon	1 tsp
1 mL	nutmeg	¼ tsp
1 mL	cloves	¼ tsp
300 mL	milk	1¼ cups
110 g	butter or margarine, melted	½ cup

Baking:

some	vegetable oil	some

Dusting:

some	icing sugar, sifted	some

PREHEAT a waffle iron.

IN a mixing bowl, beat eggs, sugar and vanilla sugar until thick.

IN another mixing bowl, combine flour, baking powder, salt and spices.

ADD flour mixture to sugar mixture alternately with milk. Stir gently but thoroughly.

FOLD in butter.

BRUSH surface of waffle iron with oil.

POUR a thin layer of batter on the iron.

CLOSE iron and bake waffles until golden yellow on both sides.

SPRINKLE waffles with icing sugar.

SERVE with applesauce, strawberries and whipped cream or ice cream.

Nutty Waffles

Recipe No. 673

Ingredients:

2	eggs, separated	2	
50 g	sugar	1/4 cup	
1 pkg	**oetker** vanilla sugar	1 pkg	
110 g	butter or margarine, melted	1/2 cup	
325 mL	milk	1 1/3 cups	
50 mL	rum	1/4 cup	
280 g	all-purpose flour	2 cups	
10 mL	**oetker** baking powder	2 tsp	
50 g	pecans, ground	1/2 cup	

Baking:

some vegetable oil   some

Sprinkling:

some icing sugar, sifted   some

Decoration:

some fresh seasonal berries   some

Fruit Sauce:

250 mL	fresh or frozen raspberries, thawed, drained and pureed	1 cup	
15 mL	sugar	1 tbsp	

Nut Cream:

125 mL	whipping cream	1/2 cup	
1 pkg	**oetker** vanilla sugar	1 pkg	
30 g	pecans, ground	1/4 cup	

PREHEAT a waffle iron.
IN a mixing bowl, beat egg yolks, sugar, vanilla sugar, butter or margarine, milk and rum.
IN another bowl mix together flour and baking powder.
ADD flour mixture to sugar mixture.
BEAT egg whites to stiff peaks. Fold egg whites and pecans into batter.
BRUSH surface of waffle iron with oil.
POUR a thin layer of batter on the iron.
CLOSE iron and bake waffles until golden yellow on both sides.
REMOVE waffles from iron. Cool completely.
SPRINKLE with icing sugar.
SERVE with fruit sauce or nut cream.

Fruit Sauce:
IN a bowl combine raspberries and sugar. Mix thoroughly with an electric mixer.

Nut Cream:
BEAT whipping cream and vanilla sugar to stiff peaks.
FOLD in pecans, gently but thoroughly.

Jam Prints

Recipe No. 674

Dough:

150 g	butter or margarine, softened	²/₃	cup
50 g	sugar	¹/₄	cup
4 drops	**oetker** vanilla flavouring concentrate	4	drops
1	egg	1	
1	egg yolk	1	
100 g	all-purpose flour	³/₄	cup
pinch	salt		pinch
100 g	hazelnuts, ground	1	cup

Brushing:

1	egg white, beaten	1	

Sprinkling:

30 g	almonds, sliced	¹/₃	cup

Filling:

125 mL	raspberry jam	¹/₂	cup

IN a mixing bowl, combine butter or margarine, sugar, and flavouring.
BEAT until fluffy.
ADD egg and egg yolk. Beat well.
MIX together flour, salt and hazelnuts. Fold into butter mixture gently but thoroughly.
CHILL for one-half hour.
PREHEAT oven to 180°C (350°F).
SHAPE dough into 2.5 cm (1") balls. Press down centres with thumb.
PLACE on baking sheet.
BRUSH with egg white.
SPRINKLE with almonds.
BAKE for 12 minutes. Remove from baking sheet.
COOL completely. Fill centres with jam.

Cheesy Crescents

Recipe No. 675

Pastry:
| ¹/₂ pkg | frozen puff pastry | ¹/₂ pkg |

Brushing:
| 1 | egg, beaten | 1 |

Sprinkling:
| 80 g | emmenthal cheese, grated | 1 cup |
| some | salt, paprika | some |

PREHEAT oven to 200°C (400°F).
THAW puff pastry according to package directions.
ROLL out pastry thinly.
BRUSH with egg.
MIX cheese with salt and paprika, to taste.
SPRINKLE over pastry.
USING a cookie cutter, cut out crescent shapes.
PLACE crescents on baking sheet.
SPRINKLE with paprika.
BAKE for 8-10 minutes.

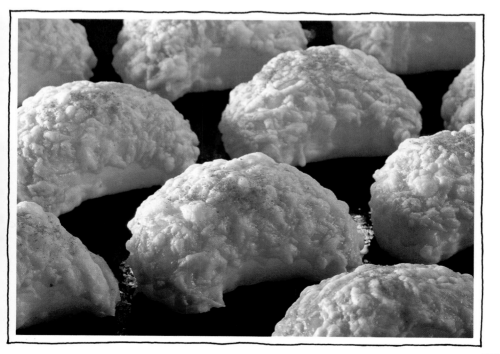

119

*Q*uark Savouries

Recipe No. 676

Dough:

150 g	all-purpose flour	1¼	cups
10 mL	**oetker** baking powder	2	tsp
2 mL	salt	½	tsp
125 g	quark	½	cup
110 g	butter or margarine, cold	½	cup

Brushing:

30 mL	milk	2	tbsp

Sprinkling:

60 mL	parmesan cheese, grated	4	tbsp
	caraway or poppy seeds		

LIGHTLY grease a baking sheet.
MIX together flour and baking powder. Sift onto a working surface.
MAKE a well in the centre. Put salt and quark in the well.
CUT butter or margarine in small pieces over the ingredients in the well.
COVER with flour.
STARTING from the centre, work all ingredients into a smooth dough.
CHILL for 20 minutes.
PREHEAT oven to 190°C (375°F).
ROLL out dough 3 mm (¹/₈") thick.
USING a variety of cookie cutters, cut out shapes.
PLACE shapes on prepared baking sheet.
BRUSH with milk.
SPRINKLE with parmesan cheese, caraway or poppy seeds.
BAKE for 15 minutes.

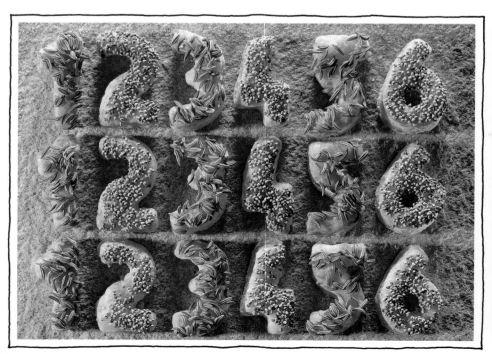

Emmenthal Treats

Recipe No. 677

Dough:

150 g	all-purpose flour	1¼	cups
1 mL	**oetker** baking powder	¼	tsp
1 mL	salt	¼	tsp
60 g	emmenthal cheese, grated	⅔	cup
1	egg yolk	1	
30 mL	whipping cream	2	tbsp
55 g	butter or margarine, cold	¼	cup

Brushing:

1	egg white, beaten	1	

Sprinkling:

100 g	emmenthal cheese, grated	1	cup
	salt, paprika, poppy seeds		

LIGHTLY grease a baking sheet.
MIX together flour and baking powder. Sift onto a working surface.
MAKE a well in the centre. Put salt, cheese, egg yolk and whipping cream in the well.
CUT cold butter or margarine in small pieces over the ingredients in the well.
COVER with flour.
STARTING from the centre, work all ingredients into a smooth dough.
CHILL for one-half hour.
PREHEAT oven to 180°C (350°F).
ROLL out dough 3 mm (⅛″) thick.
BRUSH with egg white.
USING a variety of cookie cutters, cut out shapes.
MIX cheese with salt, paprika and poppy seeds.
PRESS the biscuits, brushed side down, into the cheese mixture.
PLACE biscuits (smooth side down), on prepared baking sheet.
BAKE for 12 minutes.

*Q*uark Eclairs

Recipe No. 678

Dough:

250	mL	water	1	cup
110	g	butter or margarine	1/2	cup
1	mL	salt	1/4	tsp
135	g	all-purpose flour	1	cup
4		eggs	4	

Filling I:

55	g	butter or margarine, softened	1/4	cup
150	g	quark	2/3	cup
5	mL	fresh herbs, finely chopped (parsley, chives, cress, chervil, dill, etc.)	1	tsp
15	mL	horseradish, ground (optional)	1	tbsp

Filling II:

55	g	butter or margarine, softened	1/4	cup
150	g	quark	2/3	cup
5	mL	fresh herbs, finely chopped	1	tsp
15	mL	almonds, ground	1	tbsp
30	mL	parmesan cheese, grated	2	tbsp

PREHEAT oven to 220°C (425°F).
IN a saucepan, bring water, butter or margarine and salt to a boil.
REMOVE from heat and add flour all at once.
STIR over medium heat until mixture forms a ball around the spoon, and pulls away from the sides of the pan. (Do not overcook.)
COOL slightly.
ADD unbeaten eggs to dough one at a time, stirring after each addition until smooth.
BEAT until mixture is shiny and no longer sticky.
CHILL until mixture holds its shape.
PUT mixture into a pastry bag fitted with a star tube.
SQUEEZE desired shapes (crescents, rounds) onto an ungreased baking sheet.
BAKE for 25-30 minutes.
(Do not open oven door during first fifteen minutes of baking, pastry may collapse.)
WHILE pastries are still warm, cut in half. Let cool. Fill.

Filling I and II.

BEAT butter or margarine until fluffy.
FOLD in remaining ingredients, gently but thoroughly.
FILL bottom halves of pastries and cover with top halves.

*R*ecipe Index

	Recipe No	Page
*A*lmond Bites	644	81
Almond Boleros	600	16
Almond Boughs	607	26
Almond Buttons	621	48
Almond Linzer Cookies	611	32
Almond Raisin Rings	664	107
Almond Stars	668	111
Aniseed Biscuits	663	106
Anisettes	605	23
*B*utter Balls	647	85
Butter Cookies	596	11
Butter Rounds	629	62
*C*araway Pretzels	660	101
Caraway Seed Sticks	658	99
Cheese Puffs	655	94
Cheesy Crescents	675	119
Cheesy Spirals	654	93
Cherry Squares	610	30
Chocolate Bells	624	52
Chocolate Crescents	630	63
Chocolate Dreams	603	20
Chocolate "S"	638	74
Chocolate Stars	628	61

	Recipe No	Page
Choconut Mounds	667	110
Choco-Walnut Macaroons	594	8
Cinnamon Almond Cookies	643	80
Cinnamon Stars	671	114
Coconut Macaroons	639	75
Coffee Rounds	622	49
Craquelins	598	12
Cream Cheese Crackers	651	90
*E*asy Hazelnut Cookies	608	27
Elisen Gingerbread	645	82
Emmenthal Biscuits	657	98
Emmenthal Treats	677	121
*F*ancy Crackers	650	90
Filled Cheese Savouries	656	96
Filled Gingerbread	633	66
Filled Gorgonzola Bars	653	92
Filled Lady Fingers	599	14
Florentine Slices	613	36
Fruit and Nut Slices	640	76
*G*ingerbread Delights	626	58
Gingerbread Pretzels	635	70
Glazed Almond Rectangles	642	78
Gorgonzola Crackers	652	90

	Recipe No	Page		Recipe No	Page
*H*azelnut Half-Moons	616	40	*P*ine Nut Crescents	619	45
Honey-Almond Tartlets	602	18			
Honey Slices	632	65	*Q*uark Eclairs	678	122
			Quark Savouries	676	120
*J*am Filled Crescents	636	71			
Jam Prints	674	118	*R*ed Currant Treats	665	108
			Rum Delicacies	637	72
*L*emon Crescents	612	33			
Lemony Butter Cookies	597	12	*S*avouries	659	100
			Spicy Squares	649	87
*M*acaroon Clouds	631	64	Spicy Waffles	672	115
Marble Rings	662	105	Sultana Biscuits	615	39
Marzipan Boats	623	50	Sweet Kisses	625	54
Marzipan-Chocolate Slices	595	10			
Marzipan Filled Crescents	646	84	*T*ea Crackers	669	112
Marzipan Macaroons	618	44	Three-Cornered Hats	661	104
Meringue Rings	648	86	Train Tracks	617	42
			Turkish Treats	634	68
*N*ougat Delights	601	17			
Nutty Waffles	673	116	*V*anilla Nut Slices	666	108
*O*atmeal Cookies	670	113	*W*alnut Darlings	620	46
Oatmeal Kisses	641	77	Walnut Treats	606	24
Orange Hearts	614	38	Wine Rosettes	627	60
Orange Macaroons	609	28			
Orange Magic	604	22			

*P*ersonal Notes

*P*ersonal Notes

*T*he **oetker** *Library of Baking*

Baking is Fun — The ABC's of Baking This book will guide you through a variety of baking techniques. Learn how to prepare batters, doughs, fillings and glazes. Complete with decorating ideas and helpful hints.

Baking Is Fun — Volume 1 (Recipes No. 1 - 93) Prepare Traditional European desserts such as Black Forest Cake, Hazelnut Cream Torte and Apple Strudel with the aid of this book.

Baking Is Fun — Volume 2 (Recipes No. 94 - 190) A unique collection of European baking specialties.

Baking Is Fun — Volume 3 (Recipes No. 191 - 270) This volume consists of Traditional Holiday recipes for the Christmas season. This volume also contains a special section on recipes for diabetics.

Baking Is Fun — Volume 4 (Recipes No. 271 - 350) Light Wholesome Baking is the principal theme of Volume 4. Make a soufflé, a specialty bread or a gourmet dessert. There are many recipes to choose from.

Baking Is Fun — Volume 5 (Recipes No. 351 - 433) This volume contains a rich assortment of tempting yeast recipes.

Baking Is Fun — Volume 6 (Recipes No. 434 - 513) This volume, entitled "Specialties of the World", takes you on a culinary trip around the world with recipes from Austria to Australia and China to Sicily.

Baking Is Fun — Volume 7 (Recipes No. 514 - 593) This volume contains many Classic European recipes.

Baking Is Fun — Volume 8 (Recipes No. 594 - 678) A collection of tantalizing cookie recipes . . . from sweet to savoury. Something for every taste and temptation.

To order these books please write to:

oetker Recipe Service
2229 Drew Road
Mississauga, Ontario
L5S 1E5